THIS BOOK
BELONGS TO

PARLOR GAMES

PARLOR GAMES

AMUSEMENTS AND ENTERTAINMENTS FOR EVERYONE

CONTAINING EXPLANATIONS OF THE MOST EXCELLENT GAMES
SUITED TO THE FAMILY CIRCLE, SUCH AS—

PANTOMIMES, GAMES WITH PEN AND PENCIL,
GAMES OF THOUGHT AND MEMORY,
RIDDLES AND CONUNDRUMS AND ENIGMAS (WITH SOLUTIONS),
GAMES OF ACTION, RUSES AND CATCH GAMES,
FORFEITS, AND THE LITTLE FORTUNE-TELLER

EDITED BY ROY FINAMORE

CLARKSON POTTER/PUBLISHERS
NEW YORK

Published by Clarkson Potter/Publishers, New York, New York. Member of
the Crown Publishing Group, a division of Random House, Inc.

www.randomhouse.com

CLARKSON N. POTTER is a trademark and POTTER and colophon are
registered trademarks of Random House, Inc.

Printed in the United States of America

Design by Maggie Hinders

Library of Congress Cataloging-in-Publication Data
Parlor games: amusements and entertainments for everyone / edited by
Roy Finamore.—1st ed.
1. Indoor games.   2. Amusements.   I. Finamore, Roy.
GV1229.P285 2002
794—dc21   2002025276

ISBN 0-609-61027-9

10 9 8 7 6 5 4 3 2 1

First Edition

CONTENTS

GAMES OF THOUGHT AND MEMORY • 33

RIDDLES AND CONUNDRUMS AND ENIGMAS

(with solutions) • 65

GAMES OF ACTION • 130

RUSES AND CATCH GAMES: HAVING FOR THEIR OBJECT
TRICK AND MYSTIFICATION • 176

FORFEITS • 190

PARLOR GAMES

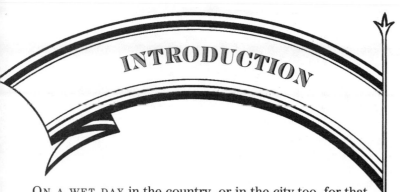

INTRODUCTION

ON A WET DAY in the country, or in the city too, for that matter, around the table following supper, or on a winter's evening at merry Christmastime, when the fire is burning cheerily, kitty purring on the hearth, and the lamps lighted, persons are often at a loss, and young folk too, sometimes, to know how to amuse themselves. Some would say, "There are books, let them read." We would whisper in their ears an adage as old as the hills, but nonetheless true or pithy; it is this: "All work and no play makes Jack a dull boy." So let us remember that as we were also once young and laughed as heartily over "Blind Man's Buff" as the youngest of our acquaintance, mirth and frolic are gifts to be had by all.

The only apparatus required in *Parlor Games* is good temper, good spirits, and gentleness, so that at any moment amusement for an evening can be obtained by anybody who wills it.

We do not wish to read our friends a homily upon politeness, as this is not a book of etiquette, but we would impress upon them that good temper is indispensable in games of any kind. We have seen the

pleasure of a whole party marred simply by the unreason-
ableness and ill humor of one of the players, who, because
he could not guess the answer to some riddle, declared that
we had cheated him, and refused to play any longer, thus
casting a gloom upon all who were playing.

Roughness, too, we would particularly caution our male
friends to avoid. Very often, when carried away by the buoy-
ancy of their spirits, they are apt to forget that ladies are
present and participating, too, in the pleasures of the game.
There is no occasion for an exhibition of strength. Men, if
you are caught, submit to it; if you are forfeited, pay the fine
without a murmur, or with a pleasant remark.

Very often a little one will spoil a game by revealing who
it is that is caught, or telling the answer to "Twenty
Questions," before the person whose turn it is to guess it has
given it up. Do not be angry with them, but take another
question, and begin again, for in all probability letting the
secret out was merely youthful enthusiasm, in knowing the
answer just as the grown members of the company. Explain
to the child that he must not do so in the future, as it spoils
the game. Take our word for it, he will try to avoid doing so
again.

We have heard many people say, "Oh, he's too young, he
can't play." We say not so; no child is too young to join in
healthy and innocent pastime. If there is no occasion to give
a child a prominent part to perform, or to perform any part
at all, you can lead him to believe that his presence is in
every way as desirable as that of the oldest person present.
Not that we advocate deception as a general thing, but we
do countenance it where it is used for the purpose of mak-

ing children happy. We ourselves have, in the game of "Fox and Goose," carried a child on our arm throughout the whole; he had nothing at all to do with it, but he laughed as loudly and heartily as any of the party.

Many of these games are very rarely found in print. They have been selected by a gentleman who is thoroughly conversant with the parlor games of America and Europe, and whose impeccable appetite for humors and frivolity assure the superior quality of the amusements contained herein.

Please consider that in some cases, as where a forfeit has to be paid by a kiss, such is only intended for a family party; in a mixed assembly, some other mode of payment can be substituted as deemed proper for company and decorum.

With these remarks, we leave our readers to enjoy themselves over *Parlor Games.*

PANTOMIMES

GENERAL DIRECTIONS. The best place for a pantomime show is where two rooms are connected by folding doors. A screen or curtain can be fitted to this opening. Care should be taken that this screen fits the opening so that no light can show over the top or around the sides or bottom. If the screen does not fit, this can be remedied by hanging some curtains or other draperies at the top and on the sides, and by putting carpets or rugs at the bottom.

Now for the screen. This is a sheet or square of muslin or light-colored calico, tacked onto a light wooden frame or to the opening. The cloth must be stretched tightly, as any wrinkles spoil the effect of the shadows. Dampen your cloth before tacking it on the frame, and then pull it as tightly as you can before tacking; when it dries, it will be found to have drawn tightly, and will be free from seams or wrinkles.

Your theater is now ready all but the light, which is prepared and used as follows:

A lamp is placed upon the floor about four feet from the center of the screen on the actors' side; the other side of the screen, where your audience sits, is, of course, in complete darkness, otherwise the shadows of the actors would not be in evidence.

Everyone not immediately engaged in the performance, but who is behind the screen, waiting for his part, must be careful to keep behind the light, so his shadow will not be thrown on the screen.

In making entrances and exits, come on from the sides, about two feet from the screen. Remember that the farther you are from the screen, and the nearer to the light, the larger will be your shadow on the screen. Remember, too, that you must be in profile, or sideways to your audience, otherwise the effect of your acting is lost; as in case you face your audience, your actions are indiscriminate and produce not the desired effect.

AERIAL FIGURES. A very funny entrance can be made by jumping over the light, which gives the appearance on the screen as if you had just dropped through the ceiling, and an exit by jumping over the light looks as if you were flying up there again in a most weird manner. A dummy figure (for example, that of a witch, riding on the conventional broom-stick) is suspended by a fine thread or wire on the side of the screen remote from the spectators. Behind this are ranged, one behind the other, and at right angles to the screen, a row of lighted candles. Being all in the same line, they throw one shadow only on the screen. The figure is now made to oscillate slightly, so as to impart some little motion to the shadow. One of the candles is now removed from its place in the row, and waved gently about, now high, now low, the effect to the spectators being that a second shadow springs out of the first, and dances about it on the screen. A second and third candle, as they leave their places in the line, produce separate shadows. It is well to have three or four assistants, each taking a candle in each hand.

SILHOUETTES. The idea of projecting silhouettes with the hands on a wall or an illuminated screen is an old one. These shadows are best made on a screen illuminated by a single lamp enclosed in a projecting apparatus. The electric light may be replaced at the amateur's house by a lamp or, better, by a candle. The candle will do very well in a small room where one can be in total obscurity except for the candle-light. The chief fault of this light for shadowgraphy is that the distance from light to screen must necessarily be short, or the shadows will not be sharp.

SHADOW PICTURES. These may be accompanied by a phonograph. Care must be taken in arranging the lights so that the shadows of the actors may be clearcut and not out of proportion to the size of the sheet on which they are thrown. The concealed phonograph starts, and presto! the shadow actors behind the sheet seem to be the very embodiment of the voices of the records. It is difficult to realize that a machine is talking. This is especially true when the impersonators are sufficiently familiar with the words as to be able to form them with their lips, although not really uttering them.

SHADOW SHOW. One of the most pleasurable forms of entertainment is the shadow show. A homemade one can be easily constructed and varied to your heart's content, if you are at all ingenious.

First, secure some light lengths of wood one inch by two inches; you will need two six feet long and two three feet long. These are to be joined together, making a frame six feet high by three feet wide.

Next, secure two more lengths one inch by one inch and three feet long, and two more lengths of the same size, but one foot long. Attach the one-foot pieces to the three-foot strips six inches from each end.

This frame is to be attached to your larger frame, twelve inches from the top.

Your framework should be joined so that it presents a flush, smooth surface at all of the joints of the two frames. Over your large framework, tack or glue black paper or muslin, leaving the opening made by the smaller frame to be covered by white muslin, making a semitransparent screen twelve by twenty-four inches, upon which are to be shown the figures.

A piece of tape is stretched across the bottom of the screen, close to the frame. This holds to the frame the figures used in the show and at the same time allows a continuation of their feet, as in a stick of some sort, to be held by the exhibitor.

By means of these continuations below the feet, the exhibitor can make the figures glide along, rock backward and forward, or suddenly disappear by pulling them downward.

All the figures should be cut out of cardboard and should have a projection or continuation of the feet. Scenery can be cut out the same way, and is quite easy, as you only need side screens. The scenes can be held by the tape strip or can be fastened to the sides by using thumbtacks. The joints of the figures are made with bits of wire. If you want the eyes of the comic figures to roll about, string a glass bead on a thread and insert in a place cut for eyes in the figure; fasten the thread at either side with a bit of glued muslin. During the performance, this screen is illuminated by placing a light about three feet behind it; the room in which the audience is seated being, of course, dark. To shut out any light that may shine out at the sides or top of the doorway, you should hang shawls or strips of your black paper muslin.

Humorous and grotesque pictures may be cut out of newspapers and magazines, pasted on cardboard, and then cut out. The show may be a pantomime, or the exhibitor may speak for the different characters. All the figures to be used should be placed on a table or a chair near the exhibitor, or held by an assistant. With a little ingenuity you can make the figures so that the arms and legs and head work on pivots, attaching them to thread so small that it will not cast a shadow on the screen. There is hardly any end to the amusement you may have in this way.

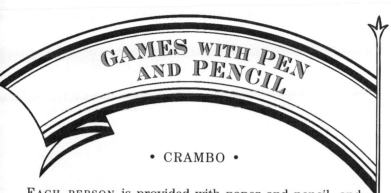

GAMES WITH PEN AND PENCIL

• CRAMBO •

EACH PERSON is provided with paper and pencil, and also with two small cards or slips of paper, upon one of which is to be written a question and on the other a single word. The questions and words are collected separately and redistributed, whereupon each player must answer in rhyme the question he has drawn, introducing into the rhyme the word on the other card. After a five-minute time limit has expired, each reads aloud the result of his labors, first giving the question and word received. To make the game more difficult, it is sometimes required that the word received shall be made a rhyming word.

Example

A player draws for his question "Where is the end of the rainbow?" and for his single word "goose." In the allotted five minutes he produces the following:

"You ask where the end of the rainbow is found;
  Just answer yourself if you can, sir.
For anser *in Latin, in English means 'goose,'*
  And I'm not such a goose as to answer."

• ILLUSTRATED QUOTATIONS •

At the top of a half-sheet of paper with which each player is provided, a picture is drawn illustrating some quotation— no matter if you are not an artist—the more absurd the picture, the better.

When all the works of art are completed, each person passes his paper to his neighbor on the right, who writes his interpretation of the picture at the bottom of the paper, folding the paper over to conceal the writing, and passing it on to the next. When each person has written on all the papers and they have again reached their original owners, they are unfolded and their contents read aloud, the correct quotation being given last of all.

For instance, a player draws a many-paned window through which is visible a face gazing at a highly exaggerated cluster of stars.

When the paper is passed to the next player to the right, that player writes as his interpretation, "In the prison cell I sit, thinking, mother dear, of you."

The next player believes it to signify "Mabel, little Mabel, with her face against the pane."

If none of the company has guessed correctly, the artist reveals to them that the picture illustrates the words from Tennyson's "Locksley Hall":

"Many a night from yonder ivied casement ere I
    went to rest,
Have I looked on great Orion sloping slowly toward
    the West."

• QUOTATIONS •

The company being seated, each member is supplied with paper and pencil. Then someone stands and gives a quotation, while all the other players write his name upon their papers, and opposite it the name of the author to whom they attribute his quotation.

After each in turn has given a quotation, the papers are collected and redistributed, care being taken that no one shall receive his own. Then each rises in turn, repeating the quotation originally given, this time adding the name of the author, while the other players meanwhile correct the papers held by them. The person who has given the largest number of authors correctly wins a prize. For example, the first player rises and says, "Colors seen by candlelight do not look the same by day."

The next says, "Handsome is as handsome does."

And so on until all have given quotations.

When the papers are exchanged, the first player, again rising, says, "'Colors seen by candlelight do not look the same by day.' Mrs. Browning."

Player 2 says, "'Handsome is as handsome does.' Goldsmith."

If any player has substituted some other name for that of Browning or Goldsmith, or has failed to write the name of any author, it must be marked as incorrect.

One person then collects and compares all the papers and announces the winner of the prize.

• LOCALIZATION OR LOCALIZED CHARACTERS •

This is distinctively a literary game, and brings into notice the great readers of the party. A long list of characters is given, who must be located in their corresponding texts.

The director of the game must have previously prepared cards or papers containing a list of characters, the number of cards to be determined by the number of guests expected.

The characters, either real or fictitious, must be chosen from books, and usually number about thirty, of course, greatly increased or lessened, according to the amount of time to be occupied. The characters should all be numbered, and a space left beside each one for the name of the book from which the character is taken.

The cards, or papers, should be handed to the guests, each of whom writes his or her name at the top of the paper. The players then write the name of the book beside each character with which they are familiar. The time should be limited according to the number of characters chosen, and at the expiration of the specified time, the cards or papers are collected. Several persons should then be chosen as a committee to mark the papers. A line is drawn through each incorrect one. The number rightly located should be added up, and placed at the top of the paper beside the name. The committee then ascertains the names of those having the highest and lowest marks.

The following is a list of characters that may be used—others, of course, may be supplemented according to the pleasure of the director:

1. Portia
2. Barkis
3. Pip
4. Sam Weller
5. Scrooge
6. Desdemona
7. Cassius
8. Max Fisher
9. Rowena
10. Arthur Shelby
11. Lady Dedlock
12. Kurtz
13. Brian Osmond
14. James Ramsay
15. Ophelia
16. Jerry Cruncher
17. Miss Sophia Grangerford
18. Rip Van Winkle
19. Priscilla
20. Hester Prynne
21. Becky Sharp
22. Micawber
23. Tess Durbyfield
24. Lady Clare
25. Meg Marmee
26. Edna Pontellier
27. Falstaff
28. Fagin
29. Uncle True
30. Queequeg

• CONFIDENCE •

Each player must have a pencil and paper and write according to the instructions of the leader:

1. Each gentleman writes a lady's name; each lady a gentleman's name.
2. Any past time.
3. The name of a place.
4. Either Yes or No.
5. Yes or No again.
6. Each gentleman writes a lady's name and each lady a gentleman's.
7. Some time to come.
8. Yes or No.
9. Yes or No again.
10. The name of a place.
11. Your favorite color.
12. Any number not exceeding ten.
13. Another color.
14. Yes or No.
15. Let each write a lady's name.
16. Let each write a gentleman's name.
17. Each another lady's name.
18. Each gentleman writes a gentleman's name, and each lady a lady's name.
19. The name of a clergyman.
20. A sum of money.
21. The name of a place.
22. A number.

When all have finished, each player must read aloud what

he or she has written without altering it, in answer to the
questions below.

1. From whom did you receive your first offer? ᴋᵗᵤ
2. When was it?
3. Where did this event take place?
4. Does he love you?
5. Do you love him?
6. Whom will you marry?
7. When will it take place?
8. Do you love him?
9. Does he love you?
10. Where does he live?
11. What is the color of his hair?
12. What is his height in feet?
13. What is the color of his eyes?
14. Is he handsome?
15. Who will be the bridesmaid?
16. Who will wait upon her?
17. Who is your sympathizing confidante?
18. Who is your rival?
19. What clergyman will marry you?
20. How much is the gentleman worth?
21. Where will you live?
22. How many servants will you keep?

• WHERE IS YOUR LETTER GOING? •

All the company being seated around the room, two people
are chosen, one for postmaster, the other for carrier.

The postmaster stations himself at the top of the room, and gives every person the name of some city, written on a sheet of paper. The carrier is blindfolded and placed in the center of the room, and the postman announces, for instance, "I have a letter to go between New York and Chicago."

As soon as the names are mentioned, the persons representing these cities must change places, the carrier at the same time trying to catch one of them. If he succeeds, and can, while blindfolded, give the name of the captured player, that player must in turn become the carrier.

Whenever the postman says, "I have letters to go all over the world," everybody must rise and change places, and if, in the general confusion, the carrier secures a seat, the person who remains standing after all the seats are taken becomes the carrier.

• SHADOW PORTRAITS •

One of the party being appointed "artist," each person in turn is seated near the wall with the shadow of his face falling in profile upon a sheet of white paper held or pinned upon the wall. The only light in the room must be a single powerful lamp, so that the shadow may be clear and distinct.

The artist traces with a pencil the outline of the shadowy face and head upon the white surface, then hands the result to an assistant, who carefully cuts out the head, and upon the back of the paper remaining, writes the name of the person represented.

After each player has been thus treated, the papers are fastened, one at a time, upon a dark curtain or screen, which, showing through the head-shaped openings, gives them the appearance of silhouettes. The company is then called upon to guess the names of the originals.

• THE ANT AND THE CRICKET •

One person being appointed to represent the Cricket seats himself in the midst of the other players, who are the Ants, and writes upon a piece of paper the name of a certain grain, whatever kind he pleases.

He then addresses the first Ant: "My dear neighbor, I am very hungry, and have come to you for aid. What will you give me?"

"A grain of rice," "a kernel of corn," "a worm," etc., replies the Ant, as he sees fit.

The Cricket asks each in turn, and if one of them announces as his gift the word already written upon the paper, the Cricket declares himself satisfied and changes places with the Ant.

If the required word is not spoken, however, the same Cricket keeps his place, scorning each article of food as it is suggested to him.

In either case, the form of the question changes, and the supplicant says: "My hunger is appeased and now I wish to dance. What dance do you advise?" He therefore writes the name of a dance upon his paper and the Ants advise in turn "a polka," "a fandango," "a minuet," etc., and the game continues as before.

The third Cricket declares himself unable to dance without music, and requests that a suitable instrument be recommended. "A lyre," "a kazoo," "a mandolin," etc., say the Ants.

The fourth Cricket, tired of dancing, wishes to rest, and asks upon what he shall take his repose—"a rose-leaf," "moss," "the heart of a lily," are all suggested, but unless the word he has previously written upon his paper is mentioned, he expresses himself dissatisfied.

The fifth and last Cricket confesses fear lest while sleeping he shall be devoured by a bird, but requests advice concerning the choice of a destroyer—"a lark," "a turtle-dove," "a pigeon," are thereupon mentioned by the Ants.

By carefully selecting the most uncommon names for replies, the same Cricket may keep his place through the entire set of questions. If the word written upon his paper, however, is mentioned in any case, he must show it to the Ant, to whom he cedes his place.

• ACROSTICS •

Whoever begins the play announces that he has just returned from market, where he has bought a certain object that he names; the name must be composed of as many letters as there are players, besides the "buyer."

He then demands of each player what he will give for one of the letters of the name of the purchased object.

Supplied with pencil and paper, he writes down the offers, which must always commence with the letter he desires to trade.

When all the offers are received, he reads them aloud, and announces the use to which he will put each object offered.

Example

(For a company of eight persons.) "I have been to market, where I bought a serpent, but I wish to trade it. (Addressing the first player) What will you give me for the *S*?"

The player addressed makes his offer, and the buyer writes it down, as he does also the offers of the other players, then he says, "I am offered in trade for my

S, a Scythe;

E, an Elephant;

R, a Rope;

P, a Potato;

E, an Encyclopedia;

N, a Necktie;

T, a Trunk.

"I accept all, and this is the use I will make of them: Wishing to travel, I will search out in my Encyclopedia the countries I will visit, then I will mount my Elephant, which I shall guide with a Rope tied to his Trunk, and wearing my Necktie, and with my Scythe for a weapon, will seek the lands where the Potato grows."

This story finished, each of the seven other players makes a similar acrostic in turn.

• WHAT IS MY THOUGHT LIKE? •

One of the players asks the question "What is my thought like?" and is answered at random by the others in turn. These answers he writes down in the order received, and when everybody has responded he tells his thought. Then each player must give the reason why it resembles the object he has previously mentioned.

For instance, Player 1 thinks of something and asks, "What is my thought like?"

It is declared to be like "the sky," "the grass," "a teakettle," "an elephant," etc.

When he confesses that he has been thinking of a certain lady in the room, and asks why she is like the array of objects mentioned, he is told:

"She is like the sky because she is far above you."

"She is like the grass because cows are her natural enemies."

"She is like a teakettle because she sings."

"She is like an elephant because she takes her trunk with her when she travels," etc.

• VERBARIUM •

When everybody is provided with paper and pencil, a word, which is to be written at the top of each paper, is given—a moderately long word with two or three vowels is best. At a given signal each person begins to write down all the words that can be spelled from the letters forming the given word and beginning with its first letter.

Two minutes only are allowed, and everybody must stop promptly.

Player 1 then reads all the words he has written; then Player 2 reads any words he may have that Player 1 has omitted, and so on, each player keeping account of his own number of words. Then, the signal to write being given again, for two minutes the players search for words beginning with the second letter of the given word. No proper names are allowable; no letter must be repeated in the same word unless occurring twice in the given word; and no letter not contained in the given word can be employed.

Example

The word given is "Locomotive." After the two minutes have expired, Player 1 reads his words aloud. He has "lot, love, let, loom, lit, lime," etc.—ten words in all.

Player 2 has all of these and in addition reads "loot" and "late." The latter, however, is wrong, as it contains an *a*, which does not occur in the given word, so he counts but eleven.

Player 3 has "live" and "lie," which neither of the others have read, besides having nine that have been already given—so he scores eleven also.

When the signal for writing is again given, all words beginning with *o* are found.

When the whole word has been thus exhausted, Player 1 has a total of forty words, Player 2 thirty, and Player 3 twenty-eight, making Player 1 the winner of the game. If the given word is long and contains many vowels, it is often well to demand that all the words have at least two syllables.

• SLANDER •

One player goes from the room, while the leader, providing himself with pencil and paper, writes down all the remarks uttered by each member of the party, in turn, concerning the absent person. He being then recalled, the remarks are read to him while he endeavors to guess the names of their originators. If he succeeds in tracing a remark to its source, the person having uttered it must go from the room to be slandered in turn.

Example

A, who has gone from the room, is requested to return in order to hear the following from *B*, the leader:

B. "Somebody says you are untruthful."

A. "Was it Mr. *D*?"

B. "Wrong. And somebody else says you are conceited."

A. "That was surely Miss *Y*."

B. "Wrong again. Somebody also says you are a great gossip."

And so on until *A* chances to guess correctly. If he fails to do this, he must go from the room again himself.

• PARODIES •

Require every person present to write a parody upon some well-known poem or song, or in the style of a familiar writer, giving a subject to which each parody must be confined. A certain length of time being given, each player reads aloud his own production, while the others are required to tell what poem or song he had in mind. Here are two samples, on the subject of cats:

Scamper, scamper, little cat,
Where on earth can you be at?
Perched upon the wall so high,
Boots and brickbats you defy.
When the little starlets peep,
When the world is all asleep,
Then it is you take delight
Howling all the livelong night.

Or:

I awakened about midnight, just at midnight, kitten
*   dear,*
Your charming voice, like music, fell upon my
*   drowsy ear;*
Upon my drowsy ear, kitten, and I was heard to say:
"I'll poison you when it is day, dearest, I'll poison
*   you when it is day."*

• ADVICE •

Everybody being provided with a slip of paper and a pencil, each player writes a piece of advice upon the paper, which is then folded and put into a hat. When all the papers are collected, they are shuffled and drawn by the players. Each person must, before opening his paper, declare whether he considers the advice it contains as worthy of being followed or entirely unnecessary. He then reads the advice aloud. For instance, Player 1, who announces his advice as most excellent, discovers it to be "You would be greatly improved by endeavoring to overcome your unbearable conceit." Player 2, who says his advice is entirely uncalled for, finds it to read, "Do not be so recklessly generous, or you will someday come to want."

• CRITICISMS •

Give each of the players a sheet of paper and a pencil, and request him to write the title of some well-known book as near the top of the paper as possible. After this has been written, the sheet must be folded down in such a way as to conceal what has been written, and passed to the left-hand neighbor. Each one then writes upon the sheet the name of some popular author. This name is also concealed from view by again turning down the paper, which is then passed to the left. Next must be written some quotation, either in verse or prose, which would make an appropriate motto for a book. The paper must be again folded and, as before, passed to the left. Each one must now write a criticism upon the book supposed to be designated in the lines concealed from view. The papers are then collected and read aloud, the contents generally being received with great applause and laughter.

Example

Little Women
by
William Shakespeare

"'Tis better to have loved and lost
Than never to have loved at all."

Criticism

"This treatise is evidently the work of one who is master of his subject. It leads us from the unreal to the real. The work is absorbing. We especially recommend it to the young as a discipline for the mind."

• METAMORPHOSIS •

Each member of the company must be furnished with a slip of paper and pencil, and must draw at the top of the sheet the head of some animal: human being, beast, or bird. This he folds down, and passes to his next neighbor, receiving a sheet in turn, folded down in the same way. Some lines should be left below the fold to show in what part of the paper the neck is placed. To this must be attached, by the person who receives it, the body of any animal; and this must be turned down in the same way and passed on. Next

some legs must be added—two or four legs, according to
the fancy of the artist. When the papers are unfolded, the
animals prove far different from those planned by their
originators.

• THE SECRETARY •

The players sit at a table with papers and pencils, and each
one writes his own name, carefully folds over the paper to
conceal it, and hands it to one of the players previously
appointed as secretary. He distributes the folded papers,
saying "Character."

Then each one, writing out an imaginary character, hands
it again to the secretary, who, again distributing the papers,
says "Past."

Thereupon the players write an imaginary past for the
unknown person whose name heads the paper.

"Present" and "Future" are also demanded, likewise
"Fate," "Fortune," or anything that the secretary sees fit, or
circumstances may suggest. The papers, finally being collected by the secretary, are unfolded and read aloud.

Here is an example:

Jack Robinson

Character. Kind and genial, always ready to do a good
turn to a friend, even to lending him a dollar; firm in purpose and successful in all undertakings.

Past. Born of poor but honest parents, he began his illus-
trious career as a vendor of peanuts.

Present. Rolling in affluence, he snaps his fingers in the faces of his old companions and refuses to acknowledge them.

Future. As President of the United States, he will raise a general racket by increasing taxes without cause.

Fate. A blushing damsel of fifty will captivate his youthful heart and make him forever miserable.

Fortune. Three acres of land and a cow will be his all-sufficient patrimony.

• ANAGRAMS •

The following questions are written upon sheets of paper and passed to the guests, who write the answers at the right:

Ton Inventions

QUESTION	ANSWER
1. lonehepet	telephone
2. torghpilat	lithograph
3. pogamheen	megaphone
4. ahitonmegpare	cinematograph
5. clibeye	bicycle
6. lematioubo	automobile
7. vceltroa	elevator
8. yuellp	pulley
9. ratpeelgh	telegraph
10. doprote	torpedo

Ten Writers

QUESTION	ANSWER
1. Towtsect	Westcott
2. Ceknewiszii	Sienkiewicz
3. Kahrmam	Markham
4. Rrbiea	Barrie
5. Gilpink	Kipling
6. Lixcow	Wilcox
7. Enica	Caine
8. Lystoto	Tolstoy
9. Votsenens	Stevenson
10. Tubtren	Burnett

Ten Historical Names

QUESTION	ANSWER
1. Reoupcoirt	Puerto Rico
2. Pepilhinips	Philippines
3. Gunlanhigch	Li Hung Chang
4. Salavtarn	Transvaal
5. Niudloaga	Aguinaldo
6. Nesnittie	Tien Tsien
7. Netrehick	Kitchener
8. Gerreuk	Kreuger
9. Nitgaaso	Santiago
10. Monspas	Sampson

Ten Presidents

QUESTION	ANSWER
1. Nwoatsghni	Washington
2. Msdaa	Adams

3. Fejrefnos	Jefferson
4. Ajknsoc	Jackson
5. Loclnin	Lincoln
6. Trnga	Grant
7. Figraled	Garfield
8. Danlelcve	Cleveland
9. Rhsirano	Harrison
10. Cymknlei	McKinley

Ten Cities

QUESTION	ANSWER
1. Wnyekro	New York
2. Gicaoch	Chicago
3. Daelihppialh	Philadelphia
4. Sslutio	St. Louis
5. Tosbno	Boston
6. Ebramlito	Baltimore
7. Aleclndve	Cleveland
8. Fufboal	Buffalo
9. Nafsiscconra	San Francisco
10. Ticiannnci	Cincinnati

• FAMOUS LOVERS •

Pass out the following list of jumbled names of famous lovers:

QUESTION	ANSWER
1. Hurt	Ruth
2. Emoro	Romeo

3. Cap-Ill, Sir	Priscilla
4. Even I, Angel	Evangeline
5. Letuij	Juliet
6. Lonepona	Napoleon
7. Nosejihep	Josephine
8. Artapocel	Cleopatra
9. Nheel	Helen
10. Pan-So-Hot, Ac	Pocahontas

Allow a limited time in which the players are to "unscramble" the names, and present a prize to the one having the correct answers, or the answers nearest correct.

• THE LOST FLORAL BOUQUET •

Each person is supplied with a pencil and a plain white card decorated with floral seals. Each card should contain a list of flowers, the letters of which are mixed up. Allow fifteen minutes to find the flowers.

1. Sero	1. Rose
2. Lupti	2. Tulip
3. Pypop	3. Poppy
4. Niqoluj	4. Jonquil
5. Scirusans	5. Narcissus
6. Ilyl	6. Lily
7. Hmunhetyscram	7. Chrysanthemum
8. Tengimteno	8. Mignonette
9. Yachithn	9. Hyacinth
10. Rotancina	10. Carnation

11. Grhaaedyn	11. Hydrangea
12. Xpohl	12. Phlox
13. Sroperim	13. Primrose
14. Poiteherlo	14. Heliotrope
15. Etras	15. Aster
16. Tsaclemi	16. Clematis
17. Olidiagl	17. Gladioli
18. Hilada	18. Dahlia
19. Nitapostei	19. Poinsettia
20. Syanp	20. Pansy
21. Tovile	21. Violet
22. Rumnsatiut	22. Nasturtium
23. Glomaidr	23. Marigold
24. Chordi	24. Orchid
25. Kohoylclh	25. Hollyhock
26. Nagiumer	26. Geranium
27. Soscom	27. Cosmos
28. Ratesiwi	28. Wisteria
29. Oyepn	29. Peony
30. Lubbelel	30. Bluebell

• THE GAME OF CONSEQUENCES •

The players are provided with pencil and paper and instructed to write according to the directions given by the leader. The first one is told to write one or more terms descriptive of a gentleman. He does so, and then folds down the paper, so as to conceal what he has written, and hands it to the next one, who, after receiving the order, writes, folds the paper down as before, and passes it on to the next one, and so on, until the directions are used up. Then the leader reads the contents of the sheet aloud, which, from its absurdities, causes much amusement.

Assuming these might be the directions of the one acting as leader:

"Begin by writing a term describing a gentleman."

"A gentleman's name; someone you know, or some distinguished person."

"An adjective describing a lady."

"Mention and describe a place."

"Write some date or period of time when the thing might happen."

"Put a speech into the mouth of the gentleman."

"Make the lady reply."

"Tell the consequences."

"And what the world said of it."

The paper, upon being opened, we will assume to read as follows:

"The modest and benevolent William Tell met the beautiful Sarah Bernhardt at Coney Island on Christmas Day, 1930. He said, 'Darling, I am growing old,' and she replied, 'The butter is rank.' The consequences were that they were married, and the world said, 'Fudge!'"

GAMES OF THOUGHT AND MEMORY

• A NEW PROGRESSIVE GAME •

THIS GAME may be played at any number of tables, arranged in the order of progression, the winning couple at each table going on to the next and there changing partners, as in progressive euchre. The requirements for the game are several boxes of ordinary "anagram" letters, such as may be obtained at the gaming stores, and tally cards, one for each person. A small heap of these letters is placed in the center of each table, all turned carefully facedown.

Two couples play at each table, the opposite partners joining forces and counting their joint gains at each progression.

Before the bell rings as the signal to play, the hostess goes to each table and assigns to the players there a class of names, so that each table has a different class. For instance, to the head table may be given "names of cities," and to the others respectively, "men's names," "animals," "things to eat," "noted writers," "names of books," and so on. When a name has been assigned to each table, the hostess rings her bell, and immediately the first lady at each table draws and turns over a letter so that all four players may see it simultaneously. The first one of the four to name an object of the assigned class beginning with that letter wins the letter and places it to one side as his first gain. Then the next player turns up a letter, and so on in turn for the three minutes allowed at each table.

When the bell rings again, the partners at each table count together the letters they have captured, and the two having the greater number progress to the next table, or, if at the head table, remain there, while the two losers "go to the foot," as in progressive euchre. At the next table the letters are turned over on their faces once more, the class of objects to be named is changed, and on the ringing of the bell the play is continued as before. So the game goes on as long as may be desired, and prizes are then awarded to the lady and gentleman whose tally cards show the greatest number of progressions. The class of objects must be changed each time, and should be varied as much as possible. There may be names of flowers, fruits, colors, birds, fishes, heroes, articles of clothing, drinks, countries, rivers, and all the geographical divisions, magazines, colleges, and Bible personages.

The tally cards for this game may, of course, be made very attractive and amusing, and so may the prizes. At one party the first prizes were tiny silver pencils shaped like matches, having enameled ends, and accompanied by cards on which was written, "You have won the match."

The booby prizes were cheap linen alphabet books—a gentle hint for the study of the dictionary.

• CLUMPS •

Sides being chosen, a representative from each side goes from the room. After deciding upon the object to be guessed, they return, each going to his opponent's side, where he is asked questions answerable by yes or no, concerning the object selected. The side which first guesses correctly has the privilege of choosing a member from the opposing side.

Then the successful guesser of one party and the player who has most nearly approached success on the other go from the room and choose a new object.

The two parties must be separated by the length of the room and the questioning carried on in low tones, so that nothing said by one side can be heard and utilized by the other.

For instance, the object chosen is the thumb on the right hand of the Bartholdi statue.

Question. "Does it belong to the animal kingdom?"

Answer. "No."

Q. "To the mineral kingdom?"

A. "Yes."

Q. "Is it in existence now?"

A. "Yes."

Q. "Is it in America?"

A. "Yes," and so on until the shouts from one side announce a successful termination of their guessing and their right to choose one from among their opponents.

The game is continued until one side has entirely absorbed the other or the interest flags.

• TWENTY QUESTIONS •

This game is similar to Clumps, except that sides are not chosen and the two players who go from the room become the interrogators, while the remainder of the party select the object and answer the questions in turn, the two whose answers have furnished the desired clue going from the room when the object is discovered. The answers in this game not being limited to yes and no, the most difficult objects may be readily guessed in the twenty questions.

• RHYMES-ABOUT •

The company being seated as in other "round" games, the director reads from a book, or, if he prefers, recites a line of poetry to which the person addressed is bound to add another line corresponding in rhyme, measure, and sense with it, or else pay a forfeit.

The following specimens might pass muster on most occasions:

Director. "How sweet and bright you look tonight."

Answer. "Oh, yes! I know I look a fright."

D. "Will you just give me one kind look?"

A. "I'd rather read a pretty book."

D. "Oh, when you're near, how blessed am I."

A. "And when you've gone, oh, won't I cry?"
D. "Will you please tell the time of day?"
A. "Indeed, I really cannot say."
D. "Can you tell aught as red as rose?"
A. "Indeed I can; it is your nose."

• PREDICAMENTS AND REMEDIES •

The company being seated in a circle, each person whispers to his right-hand neighbor a predicament, and to his left a remedy. Then each in turn repeats aloud the combination received from the two sources.

Example

Player 1's neighbor to the left whispers, "What would you do if you were going over Niagara Falls?" while from the right he receives the charge to "Bob up serenely."

When he is called on to give his combination he says:

"I was asked what I would do if I were going over Niagara Falls. I would bob up serenely."

Player 2 says, "I was asked what I should do if a burglar entered the house. I would take a small dose of paregoric."

• CAPPING POETRY •

Anyone in the company having given a quotation of poetry, someone else must give one in return, beginning with the first letter of the last word quoted. Then anyone else has the privilege of capping this in the same way, and so on. It is best not to attempt any regularity or taking turns in this game.

Example

Player 1 commences by saying:

"Up from the meadows rich with corn, clear in the cool September morn
The clustered spires of Frederick stand, green-walled by the hills of Maryland."

The last word beginning with *M*, demands that the next quotation must have that for its first letter, and someone gives:

"'Mistress Mary, quite contrary, how does your garden grow?'
'With silver bells and cockle-shells and fair maids all in a row.'"

This provides *R* as the starting point for the next quotation, and so on.

• INTRODUCTIONS •

Give the names of a gentleman and lady, as if you were introducing them, and add another name, which in its combination will form another word, making a play upon the first mentioned names. Thus, Mr. and Mrs. Day, and Florrie Day (Florida); Mr. Terry and Miss Terry (Mystery); Dr. and

Mrs. Boon and Ba Boon (Baboon); Mr. and Mrs. Ware and Della Ware (Delaware).

• BIRDS HAVE FEATHERS •

All players seated or reclining respectively, the leader throws up his hands every time he mentions a bird or animal. The players follow him when he mentions any of the feathered genus but keep their hands upon their knees when he mentions species that have not feathers. The object of the game is to catch them unawares by naming birds that have feathers very rapidly, and quickly introducing something that has not. Thus: Chickens. (All hands up.) Ducks. (Hands up.) Eagles. (Hands up.) Cats. (The leader's hands up, but all others whose hands have been raised pay a forfeit.)

• THE STORYTELLER •

One person in the room begins to relate a story, and after telling enough to interest his hearers and arouse their curiosity, he suddenly breaks off, and throws a knotted handkerchief at some other member of the party, calling upon him to continue the narrative. This is kept up as long as possible, the more absurd and impossible the plot of the story, the better.

If anyone fails to respond upon receiving the handkerchief, he must pay a forfeit.

• ECHO •

This game consists in telling a story that a person designated as Echo interrupts whenever certain words are uttered.

The Echo has to repeat a given word whenever it occurs in the story, the words selected being those most likely to occur frequently.

For example, if a story of robbers is to be told, appropriate words for echoing would be woods, tree, road, horse, gun, robber, lady, groom, money, etc.

The person appointed to tell the story would then say:

"One morning a lady (lady) accompanied by her groom (groom), started down the road (road) upon her horse (horse) for a ride in the woods (woods). She had not gone far when a robber (robber) sprang from behind a tree (tree) and, pointing his gun (gun) at her, demanded her money (money)," etc.

A failure to echo the required word promptly is punishable by a forfeit.

• THE TRAVELING ALPHABET •

The players sit in a row and Player 1 mentions the name of some city, beginning with the letter *A*, to which he is going, and he asks of his neighbor what he shall do there. Player 2 must make an answer in which all the verbs and nouns begin with *A*. He must then name a city beginning with the letter *B*, and ask of his neighbor what he shall do there; and the answer must be given in the same way, the principal words beginning with the letter *B*. The alphabet can be gone through, to any extent desired, in the same manner.

Question. I am going on a journey to Amsterdam; what shall I do there?

Answer. Admire all articles.

Q. I am going on a journey to Baltimore; what shall I do there?

A. Be bothered by bugs.

Q. I am going to Cincinnati; what shall I do there?

A. Consult clever citizens.

Q. I am going to Dresden; what shall I do there?

A. Dance daily delightfully.

Q. I am going to Edinburgh; what shall I do there?

A. Enjoy every evening.

Q. I am going to France; what shall I do there?

A. Fan Frenchmen furiously.

Q. I am going to Germany; what shall I do there?

A. Give Germans great guns.

Q. I am going to Holland; what shall I do there?

A. Haul hay homeward.

Q. I am going to India; what shall I do there?

A. Indulge in idleness.

Q. I am going to Jersey; what shall I do there?

A. Just jump joyously.

Q. I am going to Kentucky; what shall I do there?

A. Kill kangaroos.

Q. I am going to London; what shall I do there?

A. Lie lazily on lounges.

Q. I am going to Maine; what shall I do there?

A. Murder many mosquitoes.

Q. I shall visit Niagara; what shall I do there?

A. Narrate notorious narrations.

Q. I am going to Ohio; what shall I do there?

A. Open oysters.

Q. I am going to Paris; what shall I do there?

A. Peel potatoes patiently.

Q. I am going to Quebec; what shall I do there?

A. Quietly quit quarreling.

Q. I am going to Rome; what shall I do there?

A. Receive rich Roman relics.

Q. I am going to Siberia; what shall I do there?

A. Spear seals and sell skins.

Q. I am going to Trenton; what shall I do there?

A. Take tea to the townsmen.

Q. I am going to Utah; what shall I do there?

A. Utter ugly untruths.

Q. I am going to Venice; what shall I do there?

A. Vex vain Venetians.

Q. I am going to Waterloo; what shall I do there?

A. Wage war wrathfully.

Q. I am going to Yucatán; what shall I do there?

A. Yell for yeast, yams, and yarrow.

• CHARADES •

Divide the company equally, and send half from the room, while the others remain as audience. Rooms separated by double doors or portières are best for the scene of action.

The party outside thinks of some word that can be represented in pantomime or tableau. Thus, when the doors open, will be revealed a half-dozen young girls standing in a line, while one of the acting party announces that this striking tableau represents the name of a famous orator. The audience, failing to guess, is told that Cicero (Sissy-row) is the man.

Again, just as the clock strikes ten, the doors open, revealing a lady eating an apple or any convenient edible, while a gentleman standing nearby points to the clock and then at her. This being correctly guessed to represent "attenuate" (at ten you ate), the other side goes from the room and the previous performers become the audience.

There are hosts of words which, with a little ingenuity and the aid of a dictionary, may be used. For example:

Ingratiate. (In gray she ate.)

Catering. (Kate. Her ring.)

Hero. (He row.)

Tennessee. (Ten, I see.)

Metaphysician. (Met a physician.)

One favorite word is "imitation." In this the audience is requested to reverse orders and come, one by one, to the actors, that being the only way in which the word can be suitably represented.

As each enters the room, the actors imitate his every word and gesture in a ridiculously exaggerated manner, until the word is guessed or the victim gives up in disgust to escape further ordeal.

• EARTH, AIR, WATER •

The company being seated in a circle, one of the number calls out "earth," throwing a knotted handkerchief at someone and beginning to count to ten. The person who receives the handkerchief must give the name of some animal before the ten counts are concluded, or he pays a forfeit.

He then throws the handkerchief to someone else, and so the game goes on.

If "air" is called, the name of a bird must be given; if "water," that of a fish.

A confusion of inhabitants and elements is the game's peril, for a cow would not be apt to inhabit the air, nor would a trout naturally belong to the earth.

• THROWING LIGHT •

Two of the company, having agreed upon a word with more than one meaning, exchange remarks calculated to throw light upon it, while the other players do their best to guess the word.

When any person fancies he has succeeded, instead of announcing the word, he makes a remark to indicate to the two leaders that he has discovered the secret.

If they are in doubt as to his knowing the correct word, they question him in a whisper. If he is right, he joins in the conversation with them; but if he is wrong, he has a handkerchief thrown over his head, which remains until he really divines the secret.

Example

Player 1 and Player 2 have agreed upon the word "hair"
   or "hare."

Player 1. "It always startles me to see one."

Player 2. "Well, for my part it would startle me much
   more not to see one."

Player 1. "Are you fond of them for dinner?"

Player 2. "Horrors, no! The presence of one quite takes
   away my appetite."

• ALLITERATION •

The party sit around the room. The leader begins by saying
a sentence. Each person repeats the sentence in turn. When
all have repeated, the leader adds a second sentence, and
the combination is then repeated by each in turn. Thus the
leader adds a sentence at every return to him until all ten
sentences have been repeated in the order in which they
were given. Anyone making a mistake either in omission or
mispronunciation is counted out. As the ranks are depleted,
the remaining ones are required to repeat faster. A prize is
given to the one, other than the leader, who makes no mistakes.

The sentences are given below:

1. One old ox opening oysters.
2. Two toads teetotally tied trying to trot to Trixburg.
3. Three tony tigers taking tea.
4. Four fishermen fishing for frogs.

5. Five fantastic Frenchmen fanning five fainting
   females.
6. Six slippery snakes sliding slowly southward.
7. Seven Severn salmon swallowing shrimps.
8. Eight egotistical Englishmen eating enormously.
9. Nine nautical Norwegians nearing northern Norway.
10. Ten tiny toddling tots trying to train their tongues to
    trill.

• CROOKED ANSWERS •

Seat all the players in a circle, then tell each in turn to whisper a question to his right-hand neighbor, giving a correct answer to his own question to the player at his left. In this way, everybody receives an absurd combination that is repeated aloud, after all questions and answers have been given.

For example, Player 1 says to his right-hand neighbor, "Who taught you to sing so well?" and, turning to the left, whispers as a reply, "The leader of the frog orchestra." Player 2, who heard the latter, has received from another source the question "What is your favorite dish?", so when he repeats aloud what he has heard, he says, "I was asked 'What is your favorite dish?' and received for an answer, 'The leader of the frog orchestra,'" while the player at Player 1's right says, "I was asked 'Who taught you to sing so well?' and received for an answer, 'Six bottles of hop bitters.'"

• THE GAME OF FIVE VOWELS •

The rules for playing are as follows: A member of the company asks a question of his right-hand neighbor. The answer given should be brief, suitable, and prompt, but must not include the vowel prohibited by the interrogator. For instance:

Amelia. "Charles, do you like apples? Answer me without an *a.*"

Charles. "Yes, I like them very much. Are you fond of dancing, Emily? Answer without an *e.*"

Emily. "I was always partial to it. Fred, with whom did you ride yesterday? Answer without an *i.*"

Fred. "With my father."

In this case, Fred, having used the letter *i* in "with," is compelled to pay a forfeit. The game then continues as before, until a number of forfeits are collected.

• GARIBALDI •

The leader first states that "Garibaldi detests his ease," and then solicits a gift for him from each. Each player must now make Garibaldi a gift, but must omit the letter *e* in his answer, or pay a forfeit.

Example

Leader. I am soliciting contributions for Garibaldi, who detests ease. What will you give him?

Player 1. A sword.

Leader. What will you give him?

Player 2. A belt.

Leader. Pay a forfeit; there is an *e* in belt. What will you give him?

Player 3. A gun.

Leader. What will you give him?

Player 4. A new red hat.

Leader. Two forfeits; there is an *e* in new, and another one in red. What will you give him?

Player 5. A gun.

Leader. Pay a forfeit; the same thing must not be named twice, and he has already had a gun. What will you give him?

Player 6. A troop of cavalry.

And so on, every repetition and every *e* paying a forfeit.

• GOSSIP •

The company being seated in a circle, the leader whispers to his right-hand neighbor a short anecdote, or a piece of information concerning somebody known to all the company. This the recipient repeats to his next neighbor, and so the story goes around the circle, the last person relating aloud the story as communicated to him. Invariably, this version bears little resemblance to the original.

Thus, Player 1 tells Player 2 that he has heard that Mr. Jones has presented his bill to Mr. Smith five times, and that he is about to put it in the hands of a lawyer.

By frequent repetitions, in rather muffled whispers, this makes a complete circle and reaches the final player's ears as follows:

"Mr. Jones is applying for a bill of divorce, so that he can marry Mrs. Smith, who has five children on her hands, and whose husband was a lawyer."

• GIVEN WORDS •

Every player whispers to his right-hand neighbor a single word—whatever he pleases, but the more difficult to introduce into an ordinary sentence, the better.

When everybody knows his word, one player begins by asking a question of his neighbor at the left, who is obliged in his reply to introduce the word he has previously received, as adroitly as possible, to avoid its detection by his interrogator.

If the latter cannot discover the word, he pays a forfeit.

• PROBLEM •

The leader inquires of the other players:

"I am thinking of an object in which all the following articles are combined:

"A big box (chest); two lids (eyelids); two kinds of musical instruments (drums, organs); spring flowers (tulips—two lips); an artist's necessity (palette—palate); three kinds of animals (hare, hart, calves—hair, heart, calves); two places of worship (temples); two stately trees (palms); two caps (kneecaps); an emblem of royalty (crown); carpenters' materials (nails); a number of Spanish gentlemen (tendons—ten Dons); two-thirds of a yard (two feet); a number of weathercocks (vanes—veins); part of a river (mouth); parts of knives (blades); two scholars (pupils); the top of a hill (brow); both sides of a vote (ayes and noes—eyes and nose); delicate fish and a number of smaller fish (soles and muscles); plenty of assurance (cheek)."

Of course, the answer to the problem is "The human body."

• BUZZ •

This is a very old game, but is always a very great favorite. The more the players, the greater the fun. The players sit in a circle and begin to count in turn, but when the number 7, or any number in which the figure 7 or any multiple of 7, is reached, they say "Buzz" instead of whatever the number may be. As, for instance, supposing the players have counted up to 12, the next player will say "13," the next "Buzz," because 14 is a multiple of 7 (twice 7). The next player would then say "15," the next "16" and the next would of course say "Buzz" because the numeral 7 occurs in the number 17. If one of the players forgets to say "Buzz" at the proper time, he is out. The game then starts over again with the remaining players, and so it continues until only one person remains. If great care is taken, the numbers can be counted up to 70, which, according to the rules, would of course be called "Buzz." The numbers would then be carried on as "Buzz 1," "Buzz 2," etc., up to 79, but it is very seldom that this stage is reached.

• THE BILL OF FARE •

This game is played in the same manner as "My Grandfather's Trunk" (see below), except that the articles mentioned must be confined to edibles, and the opening remark refers to an imaginary dinner.

Example

Player 1. "Today I had for dinner macaroni soup."

Player 2. "Today I had for dinner macaroni soup and paté de foie gras."

Player 3. "Today I had for dinner macaroni soup, paté de foie gras, and boeuf à la mode."

And so on, the object being, of course, to mention the longest and hardest words possible.

• THE HOUSE THAT JACK BUILT •

The players sit in a circle and someone begins by claiming to possess whatever object he may choose, the more out of the ordinary the better. For instance:

Player 1 announces, "Here is the key of Bluebeard's closet."

Player 2 adds, "Here is the string that was tied to the key of Bluebeard's closet."

Player 3 continues, "Here is the hemp that made the string that was tied to the key of Bluebeard's closet."

Player 4 goes on, "Here is the farmer that sowed the hemp that made the string that was tied to the key of Bluebeard's closet."

And so on, as long as the accumulation of objects can be remembered. A failure to give them all correctly is punishable by a forfeit.

• MY GRANDFATHER'S TRUNK •

The company being seated in a circle, Player 1 begins by saying, for instance, "I pack my grandfather's trunk with a pair of spectacles."

Player 2 continues, "I pack my grandfather's trunk with a pair of spectacles and a silk hat."

Player 3 adds, "I pack my grandfather's trunk with a pair of spectacles, a silk hat, and a dime novel." And so on, each person repeating all the articles already mentioned, besides adding a new one.

If anyone fails to repeat the list correctly, he drops out of the game, which is continued until the contents of the trunk are unanimously declared too numerous to remember.

• THE KEY OF THE KING'S GARDEN •

Each player is required, in this game, to repeat short sentences without mistake. New sentences are added to the short ones and failure to repeat without mistake calls for a forfeit.

The following phrases may be added to indefinitely:

"I sell you the key of the king's garden."

"I sell you the cord that held the key of the king's garden."

"I sell you the rat that gnawed the cord," etc.

"I sell you the cat that ate the rat," etc.

"I sell you the dog that killed the cat," etc.

"I sell you the stick that beat the dog," etc.

"I sell you the fire that burned the stick," etc.

"I sell you the water that quenched the fire," etc.

"I sell you the pail that carried the water," etc.

• THE MENAGERIE •

To each member of the company is given the name of a bird or animal by the "keeper" who is to relate a story of adventure in which the names of the birds and animals are frequently mentioned. At the mention of a bird or animal, the member of the company bearing that creature is to imitate its noise or callings. Any player failing to do so promptly, or imitating the noise of a creature assigned to someone else, is required to pay a forfeit. The "keeper" may demand the delinquent player's seat instead of a forfeit and assume his menagerie name while the unseated one becomes the "keeper" and must continue the story.

• I LOVE MY LOVE WITH AN "A" •

To play this game, it is best for the players to arrange themselves in a half-circle. Then one begins, "I love my love with an 'A,' because she is affectionate; I hate her with an 'A,' because she is artful. Her name is Alice, she comes from Aberdeen, and I gave her an apricot." The next player says, "I love my love with a 'B,' because she is bonnie; I hate her with a 'B,' because she is boastful. Her name is Bertha, she comes from Bath, and I gave her a book." The next player takes "C," and the next "D," and so on through the alphabet.

• MY AUNT HAS ARRIVED FROM PARIS •

A circle is formed, all the players kneeling on the floor. The leader says to the one on his right side, "My aunt has arrived from Paris," and the one addressed asks, "What did she bring you?" The leader answers, "A pair of scissors," and at once imitates the opening and shutting of the scissors with two fingers. This same question is asked, answered, and imitated by each one around the circle.

The leader again says, "My aunt has arrived from Paris," and the one addressed asks, "What did she bring you?" The leader, still keeping up the scissors motion, says, "A fan," and at once imitates fanning with the other hand. This goes around the circle as before.

The leader then announces in the same way, "A rocking horse," and mimics the motion by moving his body up and down, all the while remaining on his knees. This also goes around the circle.

Finally in the same manner the leader announces a cuckoo, and immediately gives the imitation of a cuckoo, which is also done in turn around the circle. All imitations are to be kept up continuously by each one until the players are exhausted. The one holding out the longest is the winner.

• THE GAME OF "IT" •

Here is a game that will amuse any party, but you must first find out adroitly whether there is at least one person in the company who has never been initiated into the mysteries. This one is chosen to leave the room, but before he goes he must be told that those in the room will select an object that he is to guess on his return. He may ask as many questions as he wishes when the time comes, one question at a time of each person consecutively, but his questions must be so worded that they may be answered by "Yes," "No," or "I don't know."

When all this has been explained, the questioner leaves the room. The leader then arranges the party in a circle, seating alternately a boy with a girl, if possible, and explaining that each person must think of the one sitting on his or her left as the object chosen, and answer all questions as if they applied to that person. You may imagine that the conflicting answers arising from such an arrangement will confuse the questioner, and much fun will be derived by those in the secret.

For instance, the questioner may ask of Player 1, who is a girl, "Has it life?" Player 1 answers "Yes." He then asks Player 2, who is a boy, "Is it pretty?" and Player 2 very naturally answers "Yes," for he is speaking of the girl at his left. Then of Player 3, who is a girl, "Is it a girl?" and Player 3, thinking of the boy on her left, answers "No."

All this throws the questioner off the track: it has life, it is pretty, but it is not a girl. So he naturally asks Player 4, who is a boy, "Is it a boy?" and Player 4 answers "No."

The questioner will now be challenged to find something with life that is pretty, and is neither a girl nor a boy, and the result will be very amusing.

Or the questioner may ask such questions as "Is its hair long?" "Does it wear short sleeves?" and so on, and all the conflicting answers will tend to prolong the game to any desired extent.

• THE INTERRUPTED REPLY •

The players place themselves in a circle. The one who commences says in a whisper to his right-hand neighbor, "Of what use is a book?" or any other article he may select.

His neighbor must answer, correctly, "It is of use to read,"

and then ask another question of his right-hand neighbor—
for instance, "Of what use is a goblet?"

The art in this game consists in so framing one's questions that they will produce answers altogether unsuited to
the preceding question. If the answer is "It is of use to drink
from," a laughable consequence ensues, for when the round
is finished, and the person who has commenced the game
has been questioned in his turn, by taking the answer of the
person on his right as a reply to the question of the person
on his left, "Of what use is a book?" the answer is "It is of
use to drink from," and so on.

• GUESSING CONTESTS •

A pumpkin, a large ear of yellow corn, a pint of peanuts in
the shell, a pound of pecans in the shell, a basket of apples,
one chrysanthemum, a large bunch of grapes, and a bough
of oak leaves, or any containers full with countable parts,
are the requisites for this entertainment. These same articles
may serve as decorations for the room during the evening.
The game is to guess the number of parts of each one of the
list, for instance:

How many grains on the ear of corn?
How many seeds in the pumpkin?
How many grapes in the bunch?
How many pecans in a pound?
How many petals on the chrysanthemum?
How many peanuts in a pint?
How many leaves on the oak bough?

How many apples in the basket?

Of course, the answers have actually been obtained beforehand, except in the case of the chrysanthemum, or any like flower, which is counted after the company have guessed.

• THE CULPRIT'S SEAT •

A semicircle is formed by the company, one being appointed the president, one the culprit, and the rest judges. The culprit is placed opposite the president upon a stool, and the president opens the court.

"Honorable judges," he says, "do you know why the accused is upon the stool of repentance?"

"We know," replies the judges.

The judges then advance successively to the president, and whisper in his ear the reasons that they choose to give him.

This done, each resumes his place, and the president says to the culprit:

"You are accused of—" (he names all the accusations). "Do you know who has complained against you for each of these offenses?"

The accused repeats one offense after the other, and names one of the judges at each accusation. If he is wrong in every case he pays a forfeit and, keeping his place upon the culprit's seat, he must answer to a new round of accusations; if he guesses a single one of his accusers, the latter takes his place, pays a forfeit, and waits to be accused in his turn.

In playing this game, it is necessary to avoid all excesses that might sour the temper, and strictly observe the rules of politeness.

• THE PAGE OF LOVE •

A pack of cards is distributed by the leader of the game, by twos and threes, equally among the players, until all but a few have been dealt out. These few reserved constitute the leader's stock. This stock he alone is at liberty to inspect, which he does when he pleases, since he takes no other part in the game than the supervision necessary to conduct it. Those who have received their cards must keep them concealed, so as not to give any advantage to their neighbors.

After the cards are all distributed, the leader says to the person nearest him, "Have you read the Page of Love?"

The player answers, "I have read the Page of Love."

"What have you seen upon the Page of Love?"

"I have seen—" (here the person names any card he fancies, provided it is not among those he holds in his own hand.)

The leader of the game inspects his stock, and if the card named is among them, the person who has named the card pays a forfeit; if it is not in the stock, then each player examines his cards, and the one who has it places it in the hands of the leader.

If the player who names the card and the one who owns

it are of different sexes, the result is a kiss between them; if of the same sex, both players pay a forfeit. Then the game continues; the one who has replied questions his right-hand neighbor, employing the phrase already given, "Have you read . . . ?" and so on, until all the cards are returned to the leader.

If a card is named a second time, the player who is guilty of this mistake pays a forfeit.

In proportion, as the cards are gradually withdrawn from the hands of the players, those who are left without any cards retire from the game.

• MY AUNT'S GARDEN •

After the company has formed a circle, the leader says to his next neighbor, "I come from my aunt's garden. In my aunt's garden are four corners."

Each of the players in succession repeats the same two phrases without adding or leaving out a syllable, under penalty of a forfeit, and at the same time losing his turn to complete the sentence.

Upon completion of the circle, the leader repeats and adds to what he said before: "In the first corner there is a geranium."

In their turn the players repeat this new phrase and that which they have already repeated, paying a forfeit for any mistake.

The leader next repeats the whole phrase and adds, "In

the second corner there is a rose; I would like to kiss you, but I dare not."

He adds after the third round, "In the third corner there is a lily of the valley; tell me your secret."

Then, after having repeated the whole of these phrases, each player, in his turn, whispers a secret into the ear of his next neighbor.

The leader adds at the end of the fourth repetition: "In the fourth corner there is a poppy; that which you told me in a whisper, repeat aloud."

As the discourse, which has now arrived at its climax, passes around the circle, each player finds himself obliged to divulge the secret he has confided to his companion, often causing considerable embarrassment.

• THE SORCERER BEHIND THE SCREEN •

The player designated the Sorcerer is hidden behind a screen or door. The rest of the company place themselves out of his sight, and the one who leads the game calls out to him, "Are you there? Are you ready?"

"Yes, begin," says the Sorcerer.

"Do you know Miss ————?" (naming one of the ladies of the company).

"Yes."

"Do you know her dress?"

"Yes."

"Her shawl?"

"Yes."

"Do you know her slippers?"

"Yes."

"Her collar?"

"Yes."

"Her gloves?"

"Yes."

"And her ring?"

"Yes."

"You know, then, everything that she wears?"

"Yes."

"Her belt?"

"Yes."

"Her fan?"

"Yes."

The questioner adds as many articles of dress as he pleases, or changes them at his pleasure. The other always answers "Yes." "Since you know her so well, tell me what article of her dress I touch," asks the questioner.

The Sorcerer undoubtedly names many articles before naming the right one, and he pays a forfeit for every mistake he makes. He also pays a forfeit when he names an article not mentioned by the questioner.

But, if acquainted with the game, he would say, "You touch Miss ———'s ring," because this is the only article before which the questioner has placed the conjunction "and," which is the word of recognition to the Sorcerer that he should know what article is touched.

When any of the players acquainted with the game wish to impose upon one of their company, previous to selecting him they choose two or three Sorcerers who know the game. The latter feign to mistake once or twice, to excite no suspicion, and as soon as the last of them has guessed rightly, that Sorcerer names as his successor the dupe at whose expense they have previously agreed to amuse themselves.

• THE BISHOP •

All select a trade or profession except one, who is the Bishop, and who addresses the others as follows: "I have just come from your house, Mr. Carpenter [or any one of the trades chosen], but you were not in; where were you?"

The player thus questioned answers, "I was at the jeweler's," (or the tailor's, etc., naming any one of the trades selected).

The player who has chosen the trade named, asks, "For what purpose?" and the other must give an answer suitable to the trade named.

For instance, if a player answers that he has been to the bookseller's, he must say, "It was to obtain books; but where were you?" The bookseller will then excuse his absence by saying, "I was at the bookbinder's," who, in turn, must ask him, "For what purpose?" when he will answer, "To have some books bound; but where were you?" Then the bookbinder must excuse himself by referring to one of the other trades selected. Every player failing to make a suitable reply to the trades named, or who states any reason previously given, must pay a forfeit.

The players may also say that they have been to the Bishop's, and when asked, "For what purpose?" they must answer, "To be married," or to make some reply suitable to a bishop's profession. When the Bishop is asked, "But where were you?" he is obliged to make an answer that suits the trade of whomever he says he was visiting.

RIDDLES AND CONUNDRUMS AND ENIGMAS (WITH SOLUTIONS)

TOWARD THE end of a long evening spent merrily in dancing and playing, it is very difficult to keep everyone amused.

Then comes the time for riddles! Resting after romps and laughter, how easy to keep guests thoroughly interested, trying to guess riddles, figure out a conundrum, or solve an enigma.

It is, however, very difficult to remember a number of good and laughable puzzles, so we will give a list of some, which will be quite sufficient to bewilder a roomful for several hours.

• RIDDLES AND CONUNDRUMS •

1. When is love deformed?
2. What is the goat-stealer's song?
3. Where is happiness found?
4. Name me, and you destroy me.
5. Why should all sober people go to rest directly after tea?

  6. What grows in winter with its root upward, and dies
      in summer?

  7. What is the first thing a gardener sets in his garden?

  8. Why is a younger brother like a fair complexion?

  9. What was the longest day of Adam's life?

10. Why is a room full of married ladies like an empty
     room?

11. What makes everybody sick but those who swallow it?

12. What is the difference between a cat and a comma?

13. Who is the first nobleman mentioned in the Bible?

14. Why is a pig like the letter *n*?

15. Why is a tradesman like a divinity student?

16. Why is a mouse like grass?

17. What would a nut say if it could speak?

18. *I'm a creature most useful, and active, and known*
    Of any that daily progress through the town.
    Take from me one letter, and yet my good name
    In spite of this loss, will continue the same.
    Take from me two letters, and still you will see
    That precisely the same as before I shall be.
    Nay, take from me three, take six, or take more,
    Yet still I continue the same as before.
    Nay, rob me of every letter I've got—
    My name you'll not alter nor shorten one jot.

19. *Art's offspring, whom nature delights here to foster,*
    Can death's dart defy, tho' not lengthen life's stage;
    Most correct at the moment when most an impostor,
    Still fresh'ning in youth as advancing in age.

20. *What is pretty and useful in various ways,*
    Tho' it tempts some poor mortals to shorten their days?
    Take one letter from it, and then will appear
    What youngsters admire every day in the year;
    Take two letters from it, and then without doubt
    You will be what it is if you don't find it out.

I

21. *In other days, when hope was bright,*
    Ye spoke to me of love and light,
    Of endless spring and cloudless weather,
    And hearts that doted linked together.

II

But now ye tell another tale—
That life is brief and beauty frail,
That joy is dead and friendship blighted,
And hearts that doted, disunited.

III

Away! ye grieve and ye rejoice,
In one unfelt, unfeeling voice!
And ye, like every friend below,
Are hollow in your joy and woe!

22. What of all things in the world is the longest and the
    shortest, the swiftest and the slowest, the most divisi-
    ble and the most extended, the most neglected and
    the most regretted; without which nothing can be
    done, which devours all that is little and ennobles all
    that is great?

23. When is a door not a door?
24. What is enough for one, too much for two, and nothing at all for three?
25. What is most like a hen stealing?
26. Why was Moses believed to wear a wig?
27. What is the difference between a cow and a broken chair?
28. What did Job's wardrobe consist of?
29. If a house is on fire, why does the piano stand the best chance of escape?
30. When is a sailor not a sailor?
31. What is black and white and re(a)d all over?
32. If a man met a crying pig, what animal would he call him?
33. Why is a postage stamp like an obstinate donkey?
34. What part of the face resembles a schoolmaster?
35. Why is a root like a farmer?
36. What is worse than "raining cats and dogs"?
37. When is a ship like a half-dressed woman?
38. Why is it that you and I must never dine together?
39. What profession is a postman?
40. Why is a clergyman unlikely to be an impartial dramatic critic?
41. What snuff-taker is that whose snuff box gets fuller the more it takes?
42. Why is anger like a potato?
43. Why does opening a letter resemble a strange way of entering a room?
44. What is that which you cannot hold ten minutes, although it is as light as a feather?

45. Why is a tavern waiter like a racehorse?
46. Why are prizefights called pitch-battles?
47. Why is the letter *s* like a furnace in a battery?
48. Why is a lover like a crow?
49. What word is that which, deprived of a letter, makes you sick?

50. *In marble halls as white as milk,*
    Lined with a skin as soft as silk,
    Within a fountain crystal clear,
    A golden apple does appear.
    No doors there are in this stronghold,
    Yet thieves break in and steal the gold.

51. *Two sisters on one day were born,*
    Rosy and dewy as the morn,
    True as a sailor to his lass,
    Yet words between them often pass.
    At morn they part, but then at night
    They meet again and all is right.
    What seldom you in nymphs discover—
    They're both contented with one lover.

52. *Though banished from Heaven and sentenced to Hell,*
    The world still contains me, and owns I excel.
    The virgin disdains me and maids disapprove,
    But both must acknowledge I'm useful in love.
    To evil I'm known, and saintships all flout me
    Yet angels and devils are nothing without me.
    To the wind I'm not useful, yet blow with the gale,

I'm nothing to women, yet much to female;
Though far from a hero, and farther from brave,
I scorn a base coward, and still am a slave.
I'm first as a lover, though nothing to kiss,
Yet married and single owe to me their bliss.
I'm cold to good nature, though warm in the soul,
I'm hardened in malice, but gentle in whole.
I'm nothing, yet all—and all must confess
Without me they're nothing, and with me they're less.

53. *I'm not what I was, but the very reverse;*
I'm what I was, which though bad is now worse.
And all the day long I do nothing but fret,
Because I can't be what I never was yet.

54. Why is the death of Socrates like the upper room of a house?

55. What do we do, when to increase the effect we diminish the cause?

56. What letter in the alphabet is most useful to a deaf woman?

57. In which month do ladies talk least?

58. Why is a cockeye like a note of interrogation?

59. Where was Humboldt going when he was thirty-nine years old?

60. Which is the most ancient of the trees?

61. What are the most seasonable clothes?

62. Why are lawyers and doctors safe people by whom to take example?

63. What is the difference between a soldier and a sailor?

64. What is the best land for little kittens?

65. At what time of life may a man be said to belong to the vegetable kingdom?

66. Which are the lightest men—Scotch, Irish, or Englishmen?

67. Which are the two hottest letters of the alphabet?

68. Why is cutting off an elephant's head different from cutting off any other head?

69. Who is the man who carries everything before him?

70. Which are the two kings that reign in America?

71. When may a man's pocket be empty and yet have something in it?

72. Why is a clock the most modest piece of furniture?

73. Why is *u* the gayest letter in the alphabet?

74. What is the worst weather for rats and mice?

75. Which is the merriest sauce?

76. Why is a cat going up three pair of steps like a high hill?

77. Why is a lead pencil like an obstinate child?

78. Why is a horse like the letter *o*?

79. Why are pen-makers incited to wrongdoing?

80. Why should we never sleep in a railway car?

81. When is a boat like a heap of snow?

82. What bus has found room for the greatest number of people?

83. Who is the first little boy mentioned in American history?

84. Why is a nabob like a beggar?

85. What sort of a day would be good for running for a cup?

86. What is the difference between a spendthrift and a featherbed?

87. Is there one bird that can sing "The Lays of Ancient Rome?"

88. What have you to expect at a hotel?

89. What comes after cheese?

90. When does a man sit down to a melancholy dessert?

91. What notes compose the most "favorite tunes," and how many tunes do they compose?

92. When may a man be said to breakfast before he gets up?

93. When is the soup likely to run out of the saucepan?

94. What is that word of five letters of which when you take away two, only one remains?

95. When are volunteers not volunteers?

96. Why is the letter *b* like a fire?

97. Why is the letter *r* a profitable letter?

98. What word may be pronounced quicker by adding a syllable to it?

99. What is the difference between a dairymaid and a swallow?

100. Which animal has the most property to carry with him when he travels, and which two have the least?

101. How many sticks go to the building of a crow's nest?

102. Why was Robinson Crusoe not alone on his desert island?

103. What is that which, the more you take from it, the larger it grows?

104. What is invisible blue?

105. Which is the most miraculous animal in the farmyard?

106. What city in Ireland is drawn more frequently than any other?

107. When does beer become eatable?

108. Who was the first postman?

109. Why are bakers very self-denying people?

110. Why is whispering in company like a forged bank-note?

111. Which constellation resembles an empty fireplace?

112. What is the last remedy for a smoky chimney?

113. What relation is that child to its father who is not its father's own son?

114. When does a cow become real estate?

115. What is the keynote to good breeding?

116. Why did Marcus Curtius leap into the gulf in Rome?

117. Why is a soldier like a vine?

118. Which is heavier, a half moon or a full moon?

119. When should you avoid the edge of a river?

120. Why must a fisherman be very wealthy?

121. If the fire-grate and fire-irons cost fifty dollars, what will a ton of coals come to?

122. Why are the fourteenth and fifteenth letters of the alphabet of more importance than the others?

123. What is the way to make your coat last?

124. Why is an alligator the most deceitful of animals?

125. Why is it impossible that there should be a best horse on a racecourse?

126. Why are chickens the most economical creatures that farmers keep?

127. When may a ship be said to be in love?

128. What relation is the doormat to the scraper?

129. What vegetable most resembles little Fanny's tongue?

130. Why is gooseberry jam like counterfeit money?

131. What is that which has never been felt, seen, or heard, has never existed, and still has a name?

132. Why is a congreve-box without matches superior to all other boxes?

133. Why is a postman in danger of losing his way?

134. What is that which comes with a coach, goes with a coach, is of no use to the coach, and yet the coach can't go without it?

135. What three letters give the name of a famous Roman general?

136. Why would it affront an owl to mistake him for a pheasant?

137. If your uncle's sister is not your aunt, what relation is she to you?

138. Of what profession is every child?

139. Why is the letter *i* in Cicero like Arabia?

140. Why is troy weight like an unconscious person?

141. Why is chloroform like Mendelssohn?

142. Why does a duck put its head underwater?

143. What wild animals may be correctly shut up in the same enclosure?

144. What makes a pair of boots?

145. What tree is of the greatest importance in history?

146. Which is the most moral food—cake or wine?

147. Why is a good resolution like a fainting lady at a ball?

148. Why is a carpenter like a languid dandy?

149. When does a donkey weigh least?

150. What is the last blow a defeated ship gives in a battle?

151. Why should a sailor be a good pugilist?

152. What had better be done when there is a great rent of a farm?

153. Why is an uncomfortable seat like comfort?

154. What two letters do boys delight in, to the annoyance of their elders?

155. What single word would you put down for 40*l.* borrowed from you?

156. When is a river like a young lady's letter?

157. Why are guns like trees?

158. Why would a pelican make a good lawyer?

159. Describe a suit of old clothes in two letters?

160. Which is the proper newspaper for the scrawny?

161. What precious stone is like the entrance to a field?

162. When is a man like frozen rain?

163. Which of the stars would be subject to the game laws?

164. How do you spell an interrogation with one letter?

165. When is a bill not a bill?

166. What pen ought never to be used for writing?

167. When is a subject beneath one's notice?

168. What trade never turns to the left?

169. What trade is more than full?

170. What tune makes everybody glad?

171. Why is electricity like the police when they are wanted?

172. When is a straight field not a straight field?

173. Why is a fishhook like the letter *f*?

174. What letter is that which is invisible, but never out of sight?

175. How would you express in two letters that you were twice the bulk of your companions?

176. Why is attar of roses never moved without orders?

177. If the Greeks had pushed Pan into the Bay of Salamis, what would he have been when he came out?

178. When is a lady's arm not a lady's arm?

179. What is that which occurs once in a minute, twice in a moment, and not once in a hundred years?

180. What is an old lady in the middle of a river like?

181. When is a fish above its station?

182. When do we witness cannibalism in America?

183. When is a boy not a boy?

184. When is a city like a ship?

185. When is a skein of thread like the root of an oak?

186. What is that which has a mouth but never speaks, and a bed but never sleeps in it?

187. What word contains all the vowels in their proper order?

188. What letter used to be distributed at tournaments?

189. When is a river not a river?

190. Why is *i* the happiest of all the vowels?

191. Why should you never employ a tailor who does not understand his trade?

192. Why are your eyes like friends separated by distant climes?

193. Why is a bad-tempered horse the best hunter?

194. What sort of a face does an auctioneer like the best?

195. Why is the letter *f* like a cow's tail?

196. What is the difference between a farmer and a seam-stress?

197. What is it of which we have two every year, two every week, and two every day?

198. How does a boy look if you hurt him?

199. What medicine ought to be given to misers?

200. Why do the regular soldiers never run away?

201. What weight or measure would no competitor wish to be?

202. What part of a car resembles a sleepy person?

203. Why is the letter *r* most important to young people?

204. Why is a healthy boy like the United States?

205. When is a book like a prisoner in the States of Barbary?

206. What wind would a hungry sailor prefer?

207. On which side of a pitcher is the handle?

208. When may a chair be said to dislike you?

209. What is that which divides by uniting and unites by dividing?

210. Why are young children like castles in the air?

211. What is higher and handsomer when the head is off?

212. Why is a proud girl like a music book?

213. Why should a man always wear a watch when he travels in a waterless desert?

214. Why are bells the most obedient of inanimate things?

215. Why are the boxes at a theater the saddest places of public amusement?

216. Why is the most discontented man the most easily satisfied?

217. Why are ripe potatoes in the ground like thieves?

218. Why is it unjust to blame coachmen for cheating us?

219. When is a thief like a reporter?

220. When is the French nation like a baby?

221. What does a lamppost become when the lamp is removed?

222. What things increase the more you contract them?

223. Why is a mother who spoils her children like a person building castles in the air?

224. When you listen to your little brother's drum, why are you like a just judge?

225. Why is a pig in the drawing room like a house on fire?

226. Why is a conundrum like a parrot?

227. Why is a dancing master like a cook?

228. Why is a watchman like a mill horse?

229. Why is money like a whip?

230. Why is a portrait like a member of Congress?

231. Why is a madman like two men?

232. Why is a man who believes in God, like one who denies His existence?

233. Of what trade is the sun?

234. Why is a racehorse like a leaky barrel?

235. Why is a monument like a proud man?

236. Why is a smith like a ferryman?

237. Why is a man's hand like a hardware store?

238. Why is a red-haired lady like a band of soldiers?

239. Why is a man on horseback like a fan?

240. Why is the gallows the last refuge of a condemned man?

241. Why is a man who runs in debt like a clock?

242. Why is a slanderer like a bug?

243. Why was Adam when he awoke like a man who has no bones?

244. Why is a boaster like a game at cards?

245. What fruit is it whose name answers to a busybody?

246. Why is a shipwrecked man like an abandoned reprobate?

247. Why is a cat on her hind legs like a waterfall?

248. Why is an unbound book like a lady in bed?

249. Why is a poor man like a seamstress?

250. Why is a drawn tooth like a thing forgot?

251. Why is that which never fails like a strong knot?

252. Why is an apothecary like a woodcock?

253. Why are the Houses of Congress like an account book?

254. Why are false wings like mushrooms?

255. Why is an impudent fellow that is knocked down, like a plain-dealing man?

256. Why is a dejected man like one thrown from a precipice?

257. Why is a fire-office like an impudent fellow?

258. Why is a man led astray like one governed by a girl?

259. Why is paper like a beggar?

260. Why is a crooked man like a partial judge?

261. Why is Death called the King of Terrors and the Prince of Peace?

262. Why is a perspective glass like time?

263. What relation is a doormat to a door?

264. What is that which is often brought to table, always cut, but never eaten?

265. Why is a jailer like a musician?

266. Why is sealing wax like a soldier?

267. Why is a key like a hospital?

268. Why is a man in the putrid fever like an abusive person?

269. Why is a condemned malefactor like the root of a tongue?

270. Why is a blind beggar like a wig?

271. Why is a brewer's horse like a tapster?

272. Why is a poor lawyer much employed, and a rich one, who has left off practice, like a phenomenon in nature?

273. Why is a drunken man like an adjective?

274. Why is a dancing master like a tree?

275. Why is a tailor like a battering ram?

276. What is that which never uses its teeth for eating purposes?

277. Why is life like a publican's doorpost?

278. Why are fixed stars like pens, ink, and paper?

279. Why is a painted lady like a pirate?

280. Why is a jest like a fowl?

281. Why is a man in a garret committing murder like a good man?

282. Where was Peter when his candle went out?

283. What relation is your uncle's brother to you, who is not your uncle?

284. Why are there three objections to a glass of brandy?

285. What class of people do I name, when I say "I can't improve"?

286. What difference is there between live fish and fish alive?

287. What step must I take to remove the letter *a* from the alphabet?

288. What is the difference between a soldier and a woodman?

289. Why is a schoolboy who has just begun to read like erudition itself?

290. Why are broken heads like a rule in arithmetic?

291. Why is a loose knot like an infirmity?

292. What is that which is lengthened by being cut at both ends?

293. Why is an avaricious man like one with a short memory?

294. What is the easiest way to swallow a door?

295. Why is a man walking to a town like one endeavoring to prevent a blow?

296. Why should ladies, squeezing wet linen, remind us of going to church?

297. Why is a huntsman like juvenile card players?

298. Why is a pair of skates like an apple?

299. Why is the sun like people of fashion?

300. Why is a surgeon like a kidnapper?

301. Why is a pious man like a sieve?

302. Why is a blacksmith's apron like a convent?

303. Which is heavier, a bargeman or a lighterman?

304. Why is a solitary person like a bricklayer's laborer?

305. Why is a man who has parted from his bed like one obliged to keep it?

306. Why are sober garments like the dress of the dead?

307. Why is a school like a garden?

308. Why is a lady embraced like a pocketbook?

309. Why is a rich man like a grocer?

310. Why is your eye like a man being flogged?

311. Why is eternity like a circle?

312. Why is a bad pen like a wicked man?

313. Why is swearing like a threadbare coat?

314. Why is a parson's gown like charity?

315. Why is a gravedigger like a waterman?

316. Why is a penny cart like the lottery?

317. What are we all doing at the same time?

318. Why is the wick of a candle like Athens?

319. I am forever, and yet was never.

320. Why is the soul like a thing of no consequence?

321. Why is a beehive like a spectator?

322. Why is a handsome woman like bread?

323. Why is a false report like a tottering house?

324. Why is a tale-bearer like a bricklayer?

325. Why is a man in the midst of troubles like a prudent man?

326. What sort of an eye can penetrate a deal-board?

327. Why is a Welshman on Saint David's Day like a foundering vessel?

328. What is that which a coach cannot move without, and yet is not of the least use to it?

329. What does a stone become in the water?

330. Why is a man in love like a lobster?

331. When is a man over head and ears in debt?

332. Why is a peevish man like a watch?

333. Why is a barrister like a poker?

334. What snuff is that, the more of which is taken, the fuller the box is?

335. What trade is the sun?

336. What is smaller than a mite's mouth?

337. What is majesty deprived of its externals?

338. Why is a passionate man like fifty-nine minutes past twelve?

339. Why is an island like the letter *t*?

340. Why is the letter *e* like London?

341. Who can see best, a blind man, or one that has not eyes?

342. If you throw a man out the window, what does he fall against?

343. What question is that to which you must answer "Yes"?

344. If a man who is carrying a dozen glass lamps drops one, what does he become?

345. What belongs to yourself, but is used more by your friends than by yourself?

346. Why is a spider a good correspondent?

347. When is the clock on the stairs dangerous?

348. Why is a tight boot like an oak tree?

349. Why is the letter *c* like a schoolmistress?

350. Why is a five-pound bank note much more profitable than five sovereigns?

351. Why is a watch like a river?

352. What is that which flies high, flies low, has no feet, and yet wears shoes?

353. When has a man four hands?

354. What trees has fire no effect upon?

355. What is the difference between a schoolmaster and an engineer?

356. A man had twenty sick (six) sheep, and one died; how many were left?

357. What is that which everybody has seen but will never see again?

358. Which is the smallest bridge in the world?

359. What four letters would frighten a thief?

360. What is that which goes from London to York without moving?

361. If all the money in the world was divided equally among the people, what would each one get?

362. If I were in the sun and you were out of it, what would the sun become?

363. Why is the steeple of St. Paul's Church, London, like Ireland?

364. Why is the emblem of the United States more enduring than that of France, England, Ireland, or Scotland?

365. What is more wonderful than a horse that can count?

366. Why is a dog's tail a curiosity?

367. Why is a city in Ireland likely to be the largest city in the world?

368. Why could they not play cards in the Ark?

369. What was born at the same time as the world, destined to live as long as the world, and yet never five weeks old?

370. When day breaks, what becomes of the pieces?

371. What did Adam plant first in the Garden of Eden?

372. Which is the strongest day in the week?

373. Why is a lover like a knocker?

374. Why is a game of cards like a timber yard?

375. An old woman in a red cloak was passing a field in which a goat was feeding. What strange transformations suddenly took place?

376. Why did William Tell shudder when he shot the apple from his son's head?

377. Spell "blind pig" in two letters.

378. Which bird can lift the heaviest weights?

379. Why is a wise man like a pin?

380. Why may carpenters reasonably believe there is no such thing as stone?

381. Why is it probable that beer was made in the Ark?

382. Why does a sculptor die horribly?

383. Which is easier to spell: fiddle-de-dee or fiddle-de-dum?

384. What is the difference between a naughty boy and a postage stamp?

385. How can a gardener become thrifty?

386. Which of the English kings has most reason to complain of his washerwoman?

387. If a bear were to go into a linen-draper's shop, what would he want?

388. What makes more noise than one pig under a gate?

389. Why was Noah a disappointed rat catcher?

390. What is the difference between a brewer and a flea?

391. When a lady faints, what figure will revive her?

392. What kind of cheese is the wisest?

393. Why is a hen sitting on a gate like a penny?

394. What did Queen Elizabeth take her pills in?

395. What is it that rises and falls, travels about and wears shoes out, but never had any shoes?

396. What magazine would be likely to give the best report of a fire?

397. What kind of vice is that which people dislike if they are ever so bad?

398. What is the best thing to make in a hurry?

399. What is the difference between a bottle of medicine and a troublesome boy?

400. Why is a lame dog like a schoolboy adding six and seven together?

401. If a church is on fire, why has the organ the smallest chance of escape?

402. Why is coffee like an axe with a dull edge?

403. When may a baseball team say its "cake is all dough"?

404. What is that which is bought by the yard and worn by the foot?

405. What cord is that which is full of knots, which no one can untie, and which no one can tie?

406. Why is a fishmonger never generous?

407. What is that which works when it plays and plays when it works?

408. What is that from which you may take away the whole and yet there will be some remaining?

409. What tree is nearest the sea?

410. What coin doubles its value by taking away half of it?

411. What trade would you mention to a short boy?
412. What plant stands for the number 4?
413. Why is an opera singer like a confectioner?
414. When does a farmer double up a sheep without hurting it?
415. What lives upon its own substance and dies when it has devoured itself?
416. Why is a dog biting his tail a good manager?
417. What thing is it that is lower with a head than without one?
418. Which is the left side of a plum pudding?
419. What letter of the alphabet is necessary to make a shoe?
420. If all the seas were dried up, what would everybody say?
421. Why is it certain that *Uncle Tom's Cabin* was not written by the hand of its reputed author?
422. Why is the snow different from Sunday?
423. If an egg were found on a music stool, what poem would it remind you of?
424. Why is a schoolmaster like a shoeblack?
425. Why is a washerwoman like a navigator?
426. Why is an author the queerest animal in the world?
427. Why is it that a tailor won't attend to business?
428. When can a horse be sea-green in color?
429. Why were gloves never meant to sell?
430. When are we all artists?
431. Why are watchdogs bigger by night than by day?
432. When is a tradesman always above his business?
433. Which is the liveliest city in the world?

434. Why is a water lily like a whale?

435. Why is a shoemaker the most industrious of men?

436. What pudding makes the best cricketer?

437. When is the best time to get a fresh egg at sea?

438. Who was the first whistler?

439. What tune did he whistle?

440. Why need a traveler never starve in the desert?

441. Why is sympathy like blindman's buff?

442. If a Frenchman were to fall into a tub of tallow, in what word would he express his situation?

443. What is bookkeeping?

444. Why is scooping out a turnip a noisy process?

445. Why are teeth like verbs?

446. What ships hardly ever sail out of sight?

447. When is an artist a dangerous person?

448. Why are tortoiseshell combs like citadels?

449. Why is the Isthmus of Suez like the first u in cucumber?

450. What motive led to the invention of railroads?

451. When is a tall man a little short?

452. What houses are the easiest to break into?

453. Why is a watch the most difficult thing to steal?

454. Why is there never anybody at home in a convent?

455. Why does a person who is not good-looking make a better carpenter than one who is?

456. What is the best tree for preserving order?

457. Why is shoemaking the easiest of trades?

458. Why is a diner on board a steamboat like Easter?

459. Why is a little man like a good book?

460. Why is a plum cake like an ocean?
461. What is the difference between a soldier and a bomb-shell?
462. When are two apples alike?
463. Spell "enemy" in three letters.
464. Which is the only way that a leopard can change his spots?
465. Why did Eve never fear the measles?
466. If a man bumped his head against the top of a room, what article of stationery would he be supplied with?
467. Which is the longest word in the English language?
468. Which is the oldest tree in England?
469. How many sides are there to a tree?
470. What is that which never asks any questions and yet requires many answers?
471. What sea would a man most like to be in on a wet day?

• ENIGMAS •

1.   *Pray what is that, which I've been told*
          (Though never told in rhyme)
          That is almost itself as old
          As Adam, or as time.

          For it's been made in early days,
          As many folks have said;

And yet is subject to decays,
And even now is made.

But, as it is a secret deep,
Yet I to tell may choose;
It is what no one likes to keep,
And no one likes to lose.

2. *I'm fram'd for use, or pleasure, or for war,*
The prince and peer and peasant me prefer:
To mode and motion I am not confin'd,
I vary with the various turns of mind:
Sometimes I skim it o'er the verdant plain,
As often bustle in the fierce campaign;
I've four supporters, yet I two support,
Who twist my arms, for I was made for sport;
A dupe to caprice, I to humor suit,
And barrier am betwixt the man and brute;
But when with fitness we do not comply,
Quarrels ensue with galling hip and thigh,
Yet strange to see th' occurrence that pass,
I'm often jumbled 'twixt the mule and ass.

3. *I daily breathe, say what you will,*
And yet I have no life;
I kindle feuds, but never kill,
Nor cause the smallest strife.

4. *I lend my assistance to all,*
To tradesmen, the merchant, and clerk;

And am too at all people's call,
Provided it's not in the dark.

I messages take far and near;
I travel all over the land,
Without any power to hear,
Or legs ev'n to walk, go, or stand.

5. *As soon as I'm for business fit,*
   My master throws me in a pit;
   And there does plunge me to and fro,
   Until a set of teeth I show,
   In number oft above a score,
   Which wood or stone can't stand before:
   Whene'er my work I do come nigh,
   I make the very dust to fly:
   I never work but with my teeth,
   Then am I not a hungry thief?

6. *Attend all ye artists, attend to my lay,*
   And to you all my properties soon I'll display.
   In wit, or in learning, in wisdom or knowledge,
   I often outshine the great dons of the college;
   For in Latin, French, Spanish, nay Hebrew and Greek,
   On proper occasions I frequently speak.
   And as to my service, a numerous train
   I help to support, and some wholly maintain.
   Yet I'm not without blame; for I cause your surprise,
   When I make false alarms, and, to fright you, tell lies!
   At all times of day I'm fondly sought after,

To some I bring grief, and to others give laughter!
Without my assistance the critic would pine;
For many consult me before they can dine.
The noblest of passions that dwell in the breast,
By what I contain is too often suppress'd.
To me politicians most ardently flock,
Who prefer my instructions to Bacon or Locke.

7. Some people by my aid work real wonders,
Whilst others only make the grossest blunders;
I always please while aiming to offend,
And make that worse which I intend to mend:
Nay, often add fresh luster to the fame
Of those I strive to load with matchless blame.
Sometimes reflect dishonor and disgrace,
Upon the person that I mean to please;
So rogues and fools, by turns, are fair and wise,
And e'en the best, by fits, what they despise;
In short, I bring the lawyer cash, attend
The politician, am the doctor's friend;
And make the parson's text say this or that,
Just as in pulpit he's disposed to prate.
But lest you miss, this I will further show,
I spring from flesh and blood, but more from you.

8. Belov'd by beggar, king, and lord,
Caressed at cottage and at court;
More dangerous than the murderous sword,
The villain's weapon, children's sport.
The laborer, oppressed with toil,

Takes me to cheer a winter's eve,
Yet those who're blessed by fortune's smile,
Of wealth and plenty I bereave.
When night revolving doth appear,
To hold her sable cheerless reign;
If I invade the gloom, what fear,
What horror strikes the rustic train.
I'm blessed and cursed, hated and loved,
Despised, detested, and approved.

9. *Sometimes I have sense,*
   Sometimes I have none,
   Sometimes I offend,
   Then you bid me begone;
   Sometimes I am merry,
   Sometimes I am sad,
   Sometimes I am good,
   Sometimes very bad;
   However, to make me,
   I cost many brains,
   Much labor, much thought,
   And a great deal of pains.

10. *In Africa once I delighted to range,*
    On the tail of my owner I fled,
    But in America experience a wonderful change,
    And instead of a tail, dress a head.

11. *We seldom touch the earth, though we always go to*
    the ground; always born together, everybody takes

*great care of us, and those who lose us are much
distressed.*

12. *Sometimes I aid the lover's cause,*
    Sometimes the soldier in the wars;
    Sometimes I with the thief conspire;
    Sometimes I'm useful at a fire;
    Sometimes the carpenters befriend,
    Sometimes the bricklayers attend;
    Sometimes the gardener takes my aid,
    Sometimes I help the painter's trade;
    And sometimes little masters try
    By me to gain a bird's nest high.

13. *I am of slight texture, but great worth; can procure
    both the necessaries and luxuries of life, and change
    into various metals at the will of my possessor.*

14. *Never still for a month, but seen mostly at night.*

15. *In spring I look gay,*
    Decked in comely array,
    In summer more clothing I wear;
    When colder it grows,
    I fling off my clothes,
    And in winter quite naked appear.

16. *A tall and slender shape I bear.*
    No lady's skin more white or fair;
    My life is short, and doth decay

So soon, it seldom lasts a day.
If in the evening brought to light,
I make my exit in the night.

17. *I'm sometimes of copper, and sometimes of tin,*
    Of iron I also am made;
    One element I always carry within,
    Of another I'm never afraid.
    For so constant they tease me, I seldom am known
    To be left by the one or the other alone.

18. *By nature's law, to me is given*
    The greatest power under heaven;
    The proudest monarchs I confine,
    Who silently themselves resign,
    And own obedience by a nod,
    To me, their more than demigod;
    So universal is my sway,
    That high and low my laws obey;
    If more of me you wish to know,
    Inquire not of the sons of woe,
    But of the weary and the gay,
    Who to me ready homage pay;
    Though while they in my power remain,
    Should you inquire, 'twill be in vain.

19. *What force or strength can't get through,*
    I with a gentle touch can do;
    And many in the streets would stand,
    Were I not as a friend at hand.

20. *Although we are but twenty-six,*
    We change to millions too;
    Although we cannot speak a word,
    We tell what others do.

21. *I've a tail like a flame,*
    Pray tell me my name?

22. *I am taken from the mine, confined in a wooden case,*
    and used by many people.

23. *I bear much, devour much, and reach from pole to pole.*

24. *I'm a creature by travelers very well known,*
    And walk on the ice, in the north frigid zone.

25. *What beauties with a grace may do,*
    What, when you're dressed, looks well on you;
    What every social man would be
    To please the present company;
    What master for a wife would give,
    On what a parson's horse might live;
    What misses use for similes,
    When fingers smart or headaches tease;
    What antiquarians gladly'd give,
    To make the former ages live;
    What some men never think too bold,
    To load their chests with ill-got gold;
    What I with pleasure would pursue,
    If you, my fair one, would prove true.

26. *From rosy gates we issue forth,*
   From east to west, from south to north,
   Unseen, unfelt, by night, by day,
   Abroad we take our airy way.
   We foster love and kindly strife,
   The bitter and the sweet of life;
   Piercing and sharp, we wound like steel,
   Now, smooth as oil, those wounds we heal.

   Not strings of pearls are valued more,
   Nor gems encased in golden ore;
   Yet thousands of us every day
   Worthless and vile are cast away.
   Ye wise, secure with bars of brass
   The double gates through which we pass,
   For, once escaped, back to our cell
   Nor art, nor man, can us compel.

27. *Come, riddling wits, say what am I,*
   Distinguished by my crimson dye;
   It's probable I'd first my rise
   From Adam and Eve in Paradise;
   In them I'll fix my pedigree,
   Their sin at the forbidden tree,
   Gave birth to shame and shame bore me.

28. *In eastern climes, where Nilus laves*
   The neighboring plains with his nutritious waves,
   I first appeared on earth, and then began

To execute my vengeance upon man,
Whom I oppress'd with wide destroying hand;
Nor could all earthly help my power withstand.
Six letters form my name—but what is strange,
In losing two, I suffer little change;
The difference this—when six I had,
Where'er my quick destroying hand I laid,
The mortal wretch was well, was sick, was dead,
Possess'd of only four, I cannot kill,
Yet I remain man's sore tormentor still.
But what's most strange, though I've two letters less,
Yet I in syllables receive increase,
Let this suffice, I dare not tell you more;
Guess the six letters and you'll know the four.

29. *There's a thing as they say,*
    That appears not in day,
    And its visits but scarcely bestows;
    And it is no surprise
    To draw it with eyes,
    Besides too a chin, mouth, and nose.

    As for body, 'tis true,
    It ne'er brings to view,
    And, believe me, I fear it has none;
    So excuse me, I pray,
    For I really can't say
    That it has either flesh, blood, or bone.

30. *When first my maker formed me to his mind,*
    He gave me eyes, but left me dark and blind;
    He formed a nose, but left me without smell;
    A mouth, but neither voice nor tongue to tell
    The world my use; yet oft the fair through me
    (Although I hide the face) do plainly see.

31. *Though you seem of me fond,*
    For my safety provide,
    And when you walk out
    Take me close by your side;
    Yet you oft use me ill,
    Which I take in good part,
    Nor ever murmur or sigh
    Though I'm stabbed to the heart.

32. *When mortals are involv'd in ills,*
    I sing with mournful voice;
    If mirth their hearts in gladness fills,
    I celebrate their joys;
    And as the lark with warbling throat
    Ascends upon the wing,
    So I lift up my cheerful note,
    And as I mount I sing.

33. *I live, although I have no lands,*
    Nor for tomorrow care at all;
    A house I have, not built with hands,
    Yet mind what often doth befall:

Stout-hearted men with keenest knives
Beset me and my hapless crew;
And if I had a thousand lives,
I must be slain and eaten too.

34. *Two legs I've got which never walked on ground,*
    But when I walk or run, one leg turns round.

35. *To king and subject I assistance lend,*
    In war a firm ally, in peace a friend;
    To their diversions am a perfect slave,
    At home submissive, but in battle brave,
    To poor and prelate I give health and ease,
    The lady, merchant, and the peasant please;
    Nay, of such general use is my employment,
    Without me, life would scarce be worth enjoyment.

36. *A hundred years I once did live,*
    And often wholesome food did give,
    Yet all that time I ne'er did roam
    So much as half a mile from home,
    My days were spent devoid of strife,
    Until at last I lost my life.
    And since my death—I pray give ear—
    I oft have traveled far and near.

37. *In these corrupt degenerate times,*
    When men are raiséd for their crimes,
    Utility I boast;

And if my path they will pursue,
By easy steps I lead them to
Possess the highest post.

There are those who, with good address,
Pursued my steps with eagerness,
And did their hopes obtain;
But finding what a ponderous weight
They had to bear, resigned it strait,
And soon retired again.

38. *To me, maids frequent visits make,*
And always come for getting's sake,
And unless I demands can pay
They discontented go away.
When they arrive with their demand
They duly take me by the hand,
Nor quit it till I promise fair
To grant the amount for which they care,
They take it home to their embrace,
And let it kiss their pretty face.

39. *Homer of old, as stories tell,*
His Iliad put in a nutshell;
But did you know what I conceal—
The fate of kingdoms' commonweal.
In me a thousand mischiefs lie,
A thousand pleasures I supply;
In me the merchant lays his dust,

In me the tradesman puts his trust:
But hold—my being to explore,
Know I'm inanimate—no more.

40. *A slave I am, of frequent use,*
    None can more varied gifts produce;
    I shield from wet the gadding fair;
    From drowning save the pampered heir;
    The mutilated soldier, I
    With shapely leg do oft supply;
    Bacchus, his soul-enlivening wine,
    Does to my fostering care consign;
    Intent the finny prey to catch,
    My motions eager anglers watch.

41. *A serio-comical being am I,*
    I'm as warm as a toast, and light as a fly.
    I am of no sex, neither female or male;
    But I'm oft between both, and though strange is the tale,
    I am of no shape, no color, no size;
    Yet I may be seen by the vulgarest eyes.
    I may also be felt, nay, sometimes I've been heard;
    Sometimes I am sought, and sometimes I am feared.
    Who most earnestly buy me, most willingly give me;
    They'll give me the moment in which they receive me.
    I'm a token of peace, and, when Joan and her dear
    Forget and forgive, I'm sure to be there.
    I was the first gift, as I think you'll believe,
    That e'er father Adam presented to Eve;
    And the humor so took, as a body may say,

That his children observ'd it to this very day;
And in China, in Guinea, and eke in Peru,
In Ireland, in Greenland, and all the world through;
Tho' in color and custom they differ so wide,
I still am the gift of a lad to his bride.

42. *Although in heaven I have a place,*
   Yet 'mong the saints and sons of grace
   You'll never find me named;
   Such is my fate, that I in hell,
   With horrid shapes and howlings dwell,
   Though not among the damned.
   Yet not to hell alone confined,
   I claim a share with humankind;
   Let Neptune boast his sea,
   While I on earth my empire fix,
   (Though not one-fourth) above one-sixth
   Of which belongs to me.
   To search me out in open day,
   Were merely labor thrown away,
   I dwell in shades and night;
   Yet while in shades you search around,
   Land, water, air, or underground,
   I'm never out of sight.
   Creatures that haunt earth, sea, or sky,
   Have no one such a shape as I,
   Of all the various throng;
   Take one hint more (though strange to say)
   You'd find that hell, (were I away)
   Would not be two yards long.

43. *Hail, ladies fair, once more I try*
   My skill in mystic truth:
   Pray then bestow a gracious smile
   Upon a simple youth.
   'Fore Adam was I date my birth,
   My origin's not known:
   But now I constitute a part
   Of every mortal man.
   When Handel lived he knew my word,
   And Haydn owned my power.
   Nay, 'twas my aid alone that bade
   Their heavenly genius tower.
   Where bloody Mars his scepter sways
   O'er plains embrued with gore.
   Here I am found, and almost rent,
   By cannon's dreadful roar.
   A part of every lady too,
   Sometimes adorned with gold!
   But one hint more and then my name
   You quickly will unfold.
   When beauteous Ceres crowns the year,
   The lands in plenty yield,
   I then to bless the farmers near,
   Am full in ever field.

44. *I never laid within a bed,*
   My lodging is against the wall;
   I've fifty eyes, yet ne'er a head:
   My name, ye Misses, can you call?
   To tell you more, my body's round,

And I am seldom out of use;
I oft in greens and roots abound,
And oft discharge a watery juice.

45. Trundle was a jolly blade,
Of courage stout and free,
Many a noble match he made,
To fight with three times three.
I'll tell you how the coast he clears,
He gets among the throng,
Then kicks and cuffs them by the ears,
And lays them all along.
Though he be short and they be tall,
He very often throws them all.

46. Can you the name of me devise?
My mouth is formed just like a bow;
A nose I have and many eyes,
From whence my tears do often flow;
I seldom weep in winter time,
Although the weather's ne'er so cold,
But when gay Flora's in her prime,
My tears you often may behold.

47. My habitation's in a wood,
And I'm at anyone's command,
I often do more harm than good,
If once I get the upper hand.
I never fear a champion's frown,
Stout things I oftentimes have done;

Brave soldiers I have oft laid down,
I never fear their sword or gun.

48. *I lived in a house of glass,*
    Where I with glorious beams was blessed;
    But such my fate, it came to pass,
    At length that I was dispossessed,
    Then being brought to open view,
    Indeed, the naked truth I'll tell,
    I was both flayed and quartered too,
    By those that loved me passing well.

49. *Firm though I am, I'm firmer still,*
    From that great cause which does me fill;
    But mortal eyes ne'er saw the face
    Of him that fills my sacred space:
    I'm formed of stone, of brick and wood,
    And visited by all the good.
    I keep one clerk, whose desk I'll own
    He uses not to write upon.
    Those brought to me, with me remain,
    And none know when they'll wake again.

50. *Great numbers do our use despise,*
    But yet at last they find
    Without our help in many things,
    They might as well be blind.

51. *In almost every house I'm seen,*
    (No wonder then I'm common)

I'm neither man, nor maid, nor child,
Nor yet a married woman.

I'm penniless and poor as Job,
Yet such my pride by nature,
I always wear a kingly robe,
Though a dependent creature.

52. *I am the terror of mankind;*
    My breath is flame, and by its power,
    I urge my messenger to find
    A way into the strongest tower.

53. *Before creating nature willed,*
    That atoms into forms should jar,
    By me the boundless space was filled,
    On me was built the first-made star.

    For me the saint will break his word;
    By the proud atheist I'm revered;
    At me the coward draws his sword,
    And by the hero I'm feared.

    Scorned by the meek and humble mind,
    Yet often by the vain possessed;
    Heard by the deaf; seen by the blind;
    And to the troubled conscience rest.

    Than wisdom's sacred self I'm wiser,
    And yet by every blockhead known;

I'm freely given by the miser,
Kept by the prodigal alone.

As vice deformed, as virtue fair,
The courtier's loss, the patriot's gains,
The poet's purse, the coxcomb's care,
Guess, and you'll have me for your pains.

54. *I am found in riches, though not in wealth,*
    In illness and sickness, but not in health.
    In a hint I lurk, but I'm never known
    In a sarcasm or sally I hold my own
    In a skillful compliment never give way
    To scandal or quarrel, although I must say
    In mischievous gossips and fights I am found,
    For in evil, not good, doth my influence abound.
    I am not pretty, but shine in pleasing.
    I'm given to loving, and hating, and teasing.
    I dwell in a mansion, a ship, or an inn;
    Indeed in the latter I choose to begin.
    I am known in your life, but not in your death,
    Though I die in a sigh, yet not in a breath.
    I am given in marriage, though single I live.
    I am not generous, yet always give.
    When you meet me double, you may rely
    I am talking Latin undoubtedly.
    When you discover me, I know
    You will jealously guard me from friend or foe.
    Though selfish I am, for I never shun
    To take every care of number one,

As the Romans styled me; when I appear
As a personal pronoun, you hold me dear!

55. *A famous dancer, born in Florence, and a pupil of*
    Duprè. He obtained great fame at the Opéra in Paris.
    His vanity was even greater than his talent, for he
    often used to say, "There are only three great men in
    Europe—I, Voltaire, and the King of Prussia!"
    (Frederick II).

    1. *An Emperor of Rome; a wicked, gluttonous, and*
       cruel man. One day, visiting the field of battle
       after his lieutenants had gained for him a victory,
       he uttered these shocking words: "The body of a
       dead enemy smells sweet!"

    2. *The English king who instituted an order of knight-*
       hood, and at the same time spoke these words:
       "Honi soit qui mal y pense."

    3. *A Grecian sage who, having paid Croesus, the rich*
       King of Lydia, a visit, that monarch, with pride,
       displayed his riches before him. The philosopher,
       instead of being struck with amazement (as
       Croesus expected) at the sight of so much magnifi-
       cence, merely remarked, "Let us account no man
       happy before his death."

    4. *The translator of the scriptures into English who*
       was condemned to be burnt for heresy. When fas-
       tened to the stake, he cried with a loud voice,
       "Lord, open the eyes of the King of England!"

    5. *A river which formed the domestic boundary of a*
       great empire. It was crossed by a celebrated man

who was leading his army thither, with this excla-
mation: "The die is cast."

6. *A country to which James II was going on an*
   unsuccessful endeavor to regain his crown, when
   the parting words of Louis XIV of France to him
   were "The best thing I can wish you is that I may
   never see you again."

7. *A famous philosopher who was unjustly accused,*
   and condemned to drink poison. His wife was
   lamenting that he had been unjustly condemned.
   "Wouldst thou rather," said he, "that my condemna-
   tion had been just?"

If each of these names
You write down as you find,
The answer is plain,
By th' initials combined.

• ANSWERS TO RIDDLES AND CONUNDRUMS •

1. When it is on one side.
2. "O, Nanny, wilt thou gang wi' me?"
3. In the dictionary.
4. Silence.
5. Because when *t* (tea) is gone, night is nigh.
6. An icicle.
7. His foot.
8. Because he is injured by the son and heir.
9. The day on which there was no Eve.

10. Because there is not a single person in it.
11. Flattery.
12. A cat has its claws at the end of its paws, a comma its pause at the end of a clause.
13. The barren fig-tree.
14. Because he makes a sty Nasty.
15. Because he studies the prophets.
16. Because the cat'll (cattle) eat it.
17. Give me none of your jaw.
18. Postman.
19. A portrait.
20. Glass.
21. Church-bells.
22. Time.
23. When it is ajar (a jar).
24. A secret.
25. A cock robin.
26. Because he was sometimes seen with Aaron (hair on), and sometimes without.
27. The one gives milk and the other gives way.
28. Three wretched comforters.
29. Because it cannot be played on.
30. When he's aboard (a board).
31. A book.
32. Pork, you pine.
33. Because the more you lick it, the more it sticks.
34. The eyelid, because it always has a pupil under the lash.
35. It shoots from the eye.
36. Hailing cabs and omnibuses.
37. When she is in stays.

38. Because *U* (you) can never come until after *T* (tea).
39. He is a man of letters.
40. Because he has taken orders.
41. A pair of snuffers.
42. He gets his grub by the plough.
43. Because it is breaking through the sealing.
44. Your breath.
45. Because he runs for the plate.
46. Because they are by two men (bitumen).
47. Because it makes hot shot.
48. Because he has an attachment to carry on.
49. Musick.
50. An egg.
51. A lady's lips.
52. The letter *l.*
53. An old maid.
54. Because it is an attic story.
55. Snuff the candle.
56. *A,* because it makes her hear.
57. February, because it is the shortest.
58. Because it is a queer eye.
59. Into his fiftieth year.
60. The elder.
61. Pepper and salt.
62. Because they practice their professions.
63. One ties his ropes, the other pitches his cent.
64. Lapland.
65. When long experience has made him sage.
66. Englishmen. In Scotland there are men of Ayr; in Ireland men of Cork; but in England are *lightermen.*

67. *K, N* (cayenne).
68. Because you don't separate it from the trunk.
69. The footman.
70. Smo-king and soa-king.
71. When it has a hole in it.
72. Because it covers its face with its hands, and runs down its own works.
73. Because it is always in fun.
74. When it rains cats and dogs.
75. Caper sauce.
76. Because she's a mountain.
77. Because it never does write (right) of itself.
78. Because "gee!" makes it go.
79. Because they make people steel pens and say they do write.
80. Because the train always runs over sleepers.
81. When it is adrift (a drift).
82. Columbus.
83. Chap. I.
84. He is an India gent (indigent).
85. A muggy day.
86. One is hard up and the other soft down.
87. Yes; they are Macaw-lays (Macaulays).
88. Inn-attention.
89. Mice.
90. When he sits down to wine (whine) and pine.
91. Bank notes, and they make for-tunes.
92. When he takes a roll in bed.
93. When there's a leek in it.
94. Stone.

95. When they are mustered (mustard).

96. It makes oil boil.

97. Because it makes rice of ice.

98. Quick.

99. One skims milk and the other skims water.

100. The elephant the most, because he carries his trunk; the fox and cock the least, as they have only a brush (the fox's tail) and a comb between them.

101. None, they are all carried.

102. Because there was a heavy swell on the beach.

103. A hole.

104. A policeman when he is wanted.

105. A pig, because he is killed first and cured afterwards.

106. Cork.

107. When it is a little tart.

108. Cadmus. He carried letters from Phoenicia to Greece.

109. Because they sell what they knead themselves.

110. Because it is uttered but not allowed (aloud).

111. The Great Bear (grate bare).

112. Putting the fire out.

113. His daughter.

114. When she is turned into a field.

115. B natural.

116. Because he thought it a good opening for a young man.

117. Because he is 'listed, trained, has ten drills and shoots.

118. The half, because the full moon is as light again.

119. When the hedges are shooting and the bull rushes out.

120. Because his is all net profit.
121. Ashes.
122. Because we cannot get on *(o, n)* well without them.
123. To make your waistcoat first.
124. Because he shows an open countenance when taking you in.
125. Because there's always a better (bettor).
126. Because for every grain they eat they give a peck.
127. When she wants a mate.
128. A slip farther.
129. A scarlet runner.
130. Because it is not currant (current).
131. Nothing.
132. It is matchless.
133. Because he is guided by the direction of strangers.
134. A noise.
135. *C, p, o* (Scipio).
136. It would be making game of him.
137. She is your mother.
138. A player.
139. It is between two *c*'s.
140. It has no scruples.
141. Because it is the greatest of modern composers.
142. For divers reasons.
143. Sixteen ounces in one pound.
144. Two boots.
145. The date.
146. Cake, because it is only sometimes tipsy, while wine is always drunk.
147. Because it ought to be carried out.

148. Because he often feels a good deal board.
149. When he is within the pound.
150. Striking her own flag.
151. Because he is constantly boxing the compass.
152. It had better be sown (sewn). (Something might be said of the tares.)
153. Because it is devoid of ease (*e*'s).
154. Two *t*'s (to tease).
155. XL-lent.
156. When it is crossed.
157. People plant them and then they shoot.
158. He knows how to stretch his bill.
159. *C, D* (seedy).
160. The weakly news.
161. A gate (agate).
162. When he is hale (hail).
163. Shooting stars.
164. *Y.*
165. When it is due.
166. A sheep pen.
167. When it is under consideration.
168. A wheelwright.
169. A fuller.
170. For-tune.
171. Because it is an invisible force.
172. When it is a rye (awry) field.
173. Because it will make an eel feel.
174. *I.*
175. *I, W* (I double you).
176. Because it is scent wherever it goes.

177. A dripping pan.
178. When it is a little bare.
179. The letter *m*.
180. Like to be drowned.
181. When it rises and takes a fly.
182. When we see a rash man eating a rasher.
183. When he is a regular buck.
184. When it is under canvass.
185. When it is full of knots.
186. A river.
187. Facetious.
188. Largesse (large *s*).
189. When it is eye-water.
190. Because it is in bliss, while most of the others are in Purgatory.
191. Because you would get bad habits from him.
192. They correspond but never meet.
193. Because he soonest takes offense (a fence).
194. One that is forbidding (for bidding).
195. It is the end of beef.
196. The one gathers what he sows, the other sews what she gathers.
197. Vowels.
198. It makes him yellow (yell "Oh!").
199. Anti-money.
200. Because they belong to the standing army.
201. The last.
202. The wheel, because it is tired.
203. Because without it we should have neither Christmas nor a new year.

204. He possesses a good constitution.
205. When it is bound in Morocco.
206. One that blows fowl and chops about.
207. The outside.
208. When it can't bear you.
209. Scissors.
210. Because their existence is only in fancy.
211. A pillow.
212. She is full of airs.
213. Because every watch has a spring in it.
214. Because they make a noise whenever they are told (tolled).
215. Because they are always in tears (tiers).
216. Nothing satisfies him.
217. They ought to be taken up.
218. Because we call them to take us in.
219. When he takes notes (i.e., bank notes).
220. When it is in arms.
221. A lamplighter.
222. Debts.
223. She indulges in fancy too much.
224. Because you hear both sides.
225. Because the sooner it is put out, the better.
226. It is farfetched and full of nonsense.
227. He cuts capers.
228. He goes his rounds.
229. It makes the mare to go.
230. It is representative.
231. He is a man beside himself.
232. He is a-theist.

233. A tanner.
234. It runs.
235. It is lofty.
236. He handles the ore (oar).
237. It has nails.
238. She bears firelocks.
239. He is mounted.
240. He has nothing else to depend upon.
241. He goes on tick.
242. He is a backbiter.
243. He was bone-less.
244. He is a brag.
245. Meddler (medlar).
246. He is a castaway.
247. She is a cat erect (cataract).
248. It is in sheets.
249. He makes shifts.
250. It is out of the head.
251. It is a certainty (certain tie).
252. He has a long bill.
253. Both contain many ciphers.
254. They are sham pinions (champignons).
255. He is down-right.
256. He is downcast.
257. It deals in assurance.
258. He is miss-led.
259. It is composed of rags.
260. He is all on one side.
261. It brings dread to the wicked and joy to the
     righteous.

262. It brings distant things near.

263. Step-fa(r)ther.

264. A pack of cards.

265. He fingers the keys.

266. It is often under arms.

267. It has wards.

268. He is foul-mouthed.

269. He is down in the mouth.

270. He is cur-led.

271. He draws drinks.

272. In one we see causes without effects, and in the other effects without causes.

273. He seldom stands alone.

274. Because of his bows (boughs).

275. He makes breeches (breaches).

276. A comb.

277. It is chequered.

278. They are stationary (stationery).

279. She wears false colors.

280. It contains a merry thought.

281. He is above committing a bad action.

282. In the dark.

283. Your father.

284. There are three scruples to a dram.

285. Mendicant (mend I can't).

286. There is *a* difference.

287. By *b*-heading it.

288. The one supports his arms, and the other's arms support *him*.

289. He is learning.

290. They are vulgar fractions.
291. It is a frail tie (frailty).
292. A ditch.
293. He is always forgetting.
294. Bolt it.
295. He is going to-ward it.
296. The belles are wringing.
297. His game runs upon all fours.
298. They have both caused the fall of men.
299. It turns night into day.
300. He trepans.
301. He is holy.
302. It keeps off the sparks.
303. A bargeman.
304. He is an odd (hod) man.
305. He is bed-ridden.
306. They are grave clothes.
307. It is a seminary.
308. She is clasped.
309. He is worth his plum.
310. It is under the lash.
311. It has neither beginning nor end.
312. It wants mending.
313. It is a bad habit.
314. It covers a multitude of sins.
315. He handles the skulls (sculls).
316. It goes upon wheels.
317. Going round.
318. It is in the midst of grease (Greece).
319. Eternity.

320. It is immaterial.
321. It is a bee-holder (beholder.)
322. She is often toasted.
323. It has a week foundation.
324. He raises stories.
325. He is care-ful.
326. A gimlet-eye.
327. He carries a leak (leek).
328. Noise.
329. Wet.
330. He has a lady in his head.
331. When he wears a wig that is not paid for.
332. He is often wound up.
333. He is often at the bar.
334. The snuff of a candle.
335. A tanner.
336. Any thing that will go into it.
337. A jest-M(a jest)y.
338. He is just going to strike one.
339. It is in the midst of water.
340. It is the capital of England.
341. A man that has not *eyes*.
342. Against his inclination.
343. "What does *y-e-s* spell?"
344. A lamp lighter.
345. Your name.
346. Because he drops a line at every post.
347. When it runs down.
348. Because it produces a corn.
349. Because it forms lasses into classes.

350. Because when you put it in your pocket you double it, and when you take it out you will find it in creases.
351. Because it doesn't run long without winding.
352. Dust.
353. When he doubles his fists.
354. Ash trees, because when they are burned, they are ashes still.
355. One minds the train and the other trains the mind.
356. Nineteen.
357. Yesterday.
358. The bridge of your nose.
359. O I C U.
360. The road.
361. An equal share.
362. Sin.
363. Because there is a bell fast (Belfast) in it.

364. *The lily may fade, and its leaves decay,*
   The rose from its stem may sever,
   The shamrock and thistle may pass away,
   But the stars will shine forever.

365. A spelling bee.
366. Because it was never seen before.
367. Because each year it is Dublin (doubling).
368. Because Noah sat on the deck.
369. The moon.
370. They go into mourning (morning).
371. His foot.
372. Sunday, because all the rest are week (weak) days.

373. Because he is bound to adore (a door).
374. Because there are always a great many deals in it.
375. The goat turned to butter (butt her), and the woman into a scarlet runner.
376. Because it was an arrow escape for his child.
377. *P-G;* a pig without an *i*.
378. The crane.
379. He has a head and comes to a point.
380. Because they never saw it.
381. Because the kangaroo went in with the hops, and the bear was always bruin.
382. Because he makes faces and busts.
383. Fiddle-de-dee, because it is spelled with more *e*'s (ease).
384. Because one you stick with a lick, and the other you lick with a stick.
385. By making the most of his thyme, and by always putting some of his celery in the bank.
386. King John, when he lost his baggage in the Wash.
387. He would want muslin (muzzlin').
388. Two pigs.
389. Because it was forty days before he saw Ar-a-rat.
390. One buys his hops and the other takes them.
391. You must bring her 2.
392. Sage.
393. Because the head is on one side, and the tail on the other.
394. In cider (inside her).
395. A football.

396. A powder magazine.

397. Ad-vice.

398. Haste.

399. One is to be well shaken and taken, the other is to be taken and shaken.

400. Because he puts down three and carries one.

401. Because the engine cannot play upon it.

402. Because it must be ground before it is used.

403. When it does not have a good batter.

404. A carpet.

405. A cord of wood.

406. Because his business makes him sell fish (selfish).

407. A fountain.

408. The word *wholesome*.

409. The beech.

410. Halfpenny.

411. Grow, sir (grocer).

412. Ivy (IV).

413. Because she deals in ice creams (high screams).

414. When he folds it.

415. A candle.

416. Because he makes both ends meet.

417. A pillow.

418. That which is not eaten.

419. The last.

420. We haven't a notion (an ocean).

421. Because it was written by Mrs. Beecher's toe (Stowe).

422. Because it can fall on any day of the week.

423. "The Lay of the Last Minstrel."

424. Because he polishes the understanding of the people.
425. Because she spreads her sheets, crosses the line, and goes from pole to pole.
426. Because his tale comes out of his head.
427. Because he is always cutting out.
428. When it's a bay.
429. Because they were made to be kept on hand.
430. When we draw a long face.
431. Because they are let out at night and taken in in the morning.
432. When he lives over his shop.
433. Berlin; because it's always on the Spree.
434. Because they both come to the surface to blow.
435. Because he works to the last.
436. A good batter.
437. When the ship lays to.
438. The wind.
439. "Over the hills and far away."
440. Because of the sand which is (sandwiches) there.
441. Because it is a fellow feeling for a fellow creature.
442. In-de-fat-i-gabble. (Indefatigable.)
443. Forgetting to return borrowed volumes.
444. Because it makes it hollow (holler).
445. Because they are regular, irregular, and defective.
446. Hardships.
447. When his designs are bad.
448. They are for-tresses.
449. Because it is between two *c*'s (seas).
450. The locomotive.
451. When he hasn't got quite enough cash.

452. The houses of bald people, because their locks are few.
453. Because it must be taken off its guard.
454. Because it is an (n)uninhabited place.
455. Because he is a deal plainer (planer).
456. The birch.
457. Because the boots are always soled (sold) before they are made.
458. Because it is a movable feast.
459. Because he is often looked over.
460. Because it has many currents (currants).
461. One goes to war, the other goes to pieces.
462. When pared.
463. F-O-E.
464. By going from one spot to another.
465. Because she'd Adam (she'd had 'em).
466. Ceiling whacks (sealing wax).
467. Smiles; because there is a mile between the first and last letters.
468. The elder.
469. Two, inside and outside.
470. The street door.
471. A dry attic (Adriatic).

• ANSWERS TO ENIGMAS •

1. A bed.
2. A saddle.
3. A bellows.

4. A pen.
5. A saw.
6. A newspaper.
7. A pen.
8. Cards.
9. A book.
10. An ostrich feather.
11. Feet.
12. A ladder.
13. A banknote.
14. The moon.
15. A tree.
16. A candle.
17. A kettle.
18. Sleep.
19. A key.
20. The alphabet.
21. A comet.
22. A pencil.
23. The sea.
24. A polar bear.
25. Anything.
26. Words.
27. A blush.
28. Plague and ague.
29. The moon.
30. A mask.
31. A pincushion.
32. A bell.
33. An oyster.

34. A wheelbarrow.
35. A horse.
36. An oak tree.
37. A ladder.
38. A pump.
39. A desk.
40. A cork.
41. A kiss.
42. The letter *h*.
43. Air, hair, ear.
44. A colander.
45. Skittles.
46. A watering pot.
47. A barrel of beer.
48. A melon.
49. A church.
50. Spectacles.
51. A cat.
52. A cannon.
53. Nothing.
54. The letter *i*.
55. Vestris (Vitellius; Edward III; Solon; Tyndale; Rubicon—crossed by Julius Caesar when leading his army to Rome; Ireland; Socrates.)

• UP, JENKINS! •

THE GUESTS seat themselves at a table, opposite sides being opponents. Each side chooses a captain. The captain on one side conceals a coin (a quarter is best) in one hand. Then, holding up both hands, he asks the other side which of his hands holds it. If the other side guess aright, the quarter is passed over; if not, the quarter remains. Thus begins the game, as follows: All the hands of the side that goes first are hidden under the table while the quarter is stealthily passed to one of the number. The captain on the other side, after a short time, calls, "Up, Jenkins!" Immediately the closed hands of that party are held high, arms being vertical. They are held in this position while the opposing party inspects them. The captain then calls, "Down, Jenkins!" Every hand comes down, palms flat on the table. The opposing party then tries to locate the quarter, assisting their captain to guess. If the guess is right, the quarter is passed over to the other side, but if the guess is wrong, all the hands that are on the table are counted and noted for a score and the quarter is retained. The same steps are repeated again until the money is located and passed over. The side trying to gain the quarter can, instead of locating it immediately, request certain ones to remove their hands from the table after the quarter is passed, which makes fewer counts against them in case of failure to locate. But if they require certain hands to remove and the money is under them, the hands remaining are counted against them, and the quarter is still retained. The side having the largest score after a pre-chosen number of rounds, of course, wins the game.

• THE KEY GAME •

This game may be played by any number of persons, all of whom, except one, seat themselves on chairs placed in a circle; the one remaining stands in the center of the ring. Each sitter must next take hold with his left hand the right wrist of the person sitting on his left. When all have, in this manner, joined hands, they should begin moving them from left to right, touching each other's right hands as if for the purpose of taking something from them. The player in the center then presents a key to one of the sitters, and turns his back so as to allow it to be privately passed to another, who hands it to a third and so on; thus the key is quickly handed around the ring from one player to another, which is easily accomplished on account of the continued motion of the hands of all the players. Meanwhile, the player in the center, after the key has reached the third or fourth player, should carefully watch its progress, and endeavor to seize it in its passage between hands. If he succeeds, the person in whose hand it is found, after paying a forfeit, must take his place in the center, and give and hunt the key in his turn; but should the seeker fail in discovering the key in his attempt, he must continue his search until he succeeds. When a player has paid three forfeits, he is out.

• HUNT THE RING •

The players stand in a circle, holding in both hands a long cord forming an endless band, upon which a ring has previously been slipped.

This ring is passed rapidly from one player to another— always concealed by the hands—while a person in the center tries to seize the hands of the person who holds it. When caught, that person takes his place within the circle.

If the circle is very large, two rings may be slipped upon the cord and two players placed in the center together.

A small key is often used instead of a ring, while still another variation is to make the concealed object a small whistle with a ring attached. When this is adopted, an amusing phase of the game is introduced.

While feigning to pass the whistle from hand to hand, it is occasionally seized and blown upon by someone in the ring as the victim is at that moment turning his back, causing him to be greatly puzzled.

• A LEAF EVENING •

This is quite an attractive manner of giving an evening of social pleasure.

Leaves are cut from green fabric to represent those of different trees and plants—two leaves of each kind being made. One is given to each lady as she enters; this she pins on her dress. Its mate is dropped into a box or basket provided for that purpose.

When the guests have all arrived, a signal is given to the gentlemen that they are to approach the receptacle containing the leaves and each one is to pick up a leaf without looking to choose. He must then search for the lady who wears a similar one, and be her escort until after refreshments are served.

The table should be decorated with leaves, and at each plate a leaf cut from white paper is placed. Each person is expected to write a rhyme on this leaf in which is mentioned the name of the leaf he wears. Before the guests leave the table, the hostess gathers up the papers containing the rhymes and reads them aloud. A vote is taken to decide upon the two best rhymes. The author of each of them receives a hot-house plant.

After refreshments are served, a blackboard is brought in. Each lady and each gentleman is led up to it blindfolded, and is first given a piece of white chalk, then a piece of red chalk, with which they are expected to draw the leaf they wear. The red chalk is to vein the white leaf. The name of each artist is written beneath the leaf. When the couples have all finished their artistic work, the blackboard presents a very amusing spectacle.

• THE FARMYARD •

The leader must go around the circle, giving to each person the name of some animal, beast, or fowl. These names he whispers to each in turn. He gives them, at the same time, two signals. When he raises his right hand, each person must make the noise peculiar to his kind of animal: the horses neigh, the cows moo, the dogs bark, the cocks crow, the geese hiss, the turkeys gobble, and so on. As soon as the leader raises his left hand, all must be silent. A forfeit is required from anyone who makes a sound after the left hand is raised.

• THE RAT HUNT •

All the players seat themselves in a circle, one of them, the Rat, being supplied with a stick, a toy, or other implement with which to make a scratching noise on the floor. The player who acts as the Cat stands up in the center. The Rat watches for an opportunity to scratch on the floor with the toy when the Cat is not looking in his direction. The latter turns quickly around to detect, and if possible to seize, the instrument from the scratcher.

The Rat, however, passes the toy to another, and so on, the next sounding it whenever Cat's attention is turned in an opposite direction. If Cat succeeds in detecting a player and seizing the toy from him, they change places, the detected Rat becoming Cat in his turn.

• THE BAG OF LUCK •

The "Bag of Luck" is a decorated paper bag suspended in a doorway at a convenient height; the players, blindfolded, are given three trials to break it with pretty ribbon-wound wands provided for the purpose. These sticks are given afterward as souvenirs of the evening. The player who succeeds in making the first hole in the bag is entitled to a prize, but all share its contents. It is usually filled with candy, but flowers may be substituted when candy is considered objectionable.

• THE CUSHION DANCE •

A large cushion is placed end upward in the middle of the floor, around which the players form a circle with hands joined, having first divided into two equal parties. The adversaries, facing each other, begin by dancing round the cushion a few times; then suddenly one side tries to pull the other forward, so as to force one of their number to touch the cushion and to upset it. The struggle that necessarily ensues is a source of great fun, causing even more merriment to spectators than to the players themselves. At last, in spite of the utmost dexterity, down goes the cushion. Someone's foot is sure to touch it before very long, and the unfortunate individual is dismissed from the circle and compelled to pay a forfeit.

• BEAN BAGS •

Make twelve or sixteen bags, six inches square, of heavy canvas and loosely fill them with beans that have been previously washed and dried to remove all dust. With these can be played a variety of games, the two most interesting of which are as follows:

I

Appoint two leaders, who choose sides, arranging the sides in lines facing each other, with a small table at each end of each line.

The bean bags being equally divided, each leader deposits his share upon the table nearest him. Then, at a given signal, seizing one bag at a time with one hand, with the other hand he starts them down the line, each player passing them to the next until they reach the last, who places them as fast as received upon the table next to him.

When all the bags have reached this table, the last player sends them back up the line to the leader, who again deposits them upon his table, with all players using but one hand.

Whichever side first succeeds in passing all of the bags down the line and back wins the round. It takes five rounds to make a game, the side winning three out of the five being successful.

The bags must be passed as rapidly as possible, and every bag must touch the end table before being returned.

If a bag falls to the ground, it is best to leave it where it falls until all the others are down the line, when it may be quickly picked up and passed on with little loss of time. But if in his excitement a player stoops at once to pick it up, he will cause a delay in passing the remaining bags, which invariably creates much confusion and loss of time.

II

Have a board three feet long and two feet wide with an opening about five inches square, elevated at one end. Station this board at one end of a long room and divide the company equally.

Eight of the bean bags are all that are required.

The leader of one side begins. Standing at a suitable distance from the board, he endeavors to throw the bags, one at a time, through the square opening. Every bag that reaches the goal counts ten, every one that lands upon the board five, and every one that falls to the ground outside of the board a loss of ten.

The sides play alternately, and after three rounds for each, the scores, which have been carefully kept by one member of the party, are balanced, and the side having the greatest gain is declared the winner.

A prize is often given for the highest individual score.

• SLIP THE RULER •

All players except one seat themselves in a row. They pass a ruler from hand to hand up and down the line. It is the duty of the one standing to try to seize the ruler. If he succeeds in doing this, the player in whose hand it was at the time changes places with him. If the players sit close together and make very rapid movements, they may succeed in baffling the searcher for a long time.

• SIMON SAYS •

In this game an imaginary Simon is the presiding genius, and the orders of no one but Simon are to be obeyed. Simon begins the game by saying, "Simon says thumbs up," upon which everyone must immediately obey the command of Simon or incur the penalty of paying a forfeit. Simon may then say, "Wink your left eye," "Shake your neighbor's hand," "Twirl your thumbs," or anything equally absurd. Whatever Simon says must be done. No command, however, not prefaced by the words "Simon says" is to be obeyed. With the idea of winning forfeits, the leader will endeavor to induce the company to do certain things not authorized by Simon. Indeed, the fun of the game consists in everyone doing the wrong thing instead of the right one, and in having to pay a number of forfeits.

• DO AS I DO •

The company sits in a circle. Player 1 begins the game by patting his hand on his knee and saying to his left-hand neighbor, "Neighbor, neighbor, how art thou?" to which Player 2 replies, "Very well, I thank thee." Player 1 then asks, "And how is the neighbor next to thee?" to which Player 2 responds, "I don't know, but I'll go see." Player 2 then turns to Player 3 and asks the same questions, and so the questions pass around the whole circle until they come back to Player 1, who, after replying, repeats the questions to Player 2, patting both knees with both hands. This form is then gone through with by the whole company; Player 1 then taps his right foot while both hands are patting knees, then adds the left foot. The next time he shakes his head, then stands up, keeping all the motions going at the same time.

This is a very amusing game, especially for small children, making noise enough and yet not being boisterous.

• SILENT JONES •

The group seat themselves so that each one can whisper to his next neighbor on his right. When all are ready, each one orders his next neighbor to do some absurd thing. When everyone has received a commission, the leader announces,

"The meeting has begun." All join hands and solemnly shake them, after which no one must speak or laugh. Each one in turn performs his commission with solemnity. Anyone who laughs or speaks pays a forfeit.

Suggestions for commissions: One might be ordered to make a pantomime speech, another to dance a jig, another to sing by action. A gentleman might be told to play barber or dentist. Another might offer to eat a nut, etc.

• FOX AND GEESE •

There must be an even number of persons in this game. A circle is formed, the players standing two by two, so that those who are on the outside each have one person in front of them; these are called the Geese, and there must be some space left between the couples, to allow the one who is chased to run in and out of the circle. Two must be left out, one a Goose, and the other the Fox. The Fox is to catch the Goose not belonging to the circle. The Goose may run around and also within the circle, but the Fox is not allowed to pass within. When the Goose who is pursued places himself before one of the couples of the circle, the one standing outside of that three immediately becomes the pursued, and must endeavor to avoid the Fox by darting within the circle and likewise placing himself before one of the couples. If the Goose is touched by the Fox while in the position of third one in a row, or if touched in passing from this third place to one of safety, he becomes the Fox instead, and the Fox becomes a Goose. The amusement of this game depends upon the spirit and animation with which it is conducted. Great rapidity of movement is necessary, especially when the Fox is a very active one, who will endeavor to dart upon the outside Goose in sudden and unexpected ways.

• HOT COCKLES •

The origin of the title of this game is lost in the mists of antiquity. A player kneeling down before a lady conceals his face in her lap, and places one hand, with the palm uppermost, on his back.

The rest of the company advances in turn, each administering a slap to the open hand, the person kneeling meanwhile trying to discover, with face still concealed, who has bestowed the slap.

When he guesses correctly, the detected player takes his place.

• FLY FEATHER •

The company sits in as small a circle as possible without crowding each other, with a sheet stretched and held tightly under each chin.

The leader takes a small downy feather—any pillow will

furnish one—and lets it float in the air, giving it a puff with his breath.

The person toward whom it descends must likewise blow it up and away, for if it falls upon him, or he allows it to fall upon the sheet, he pays a forfeit.

• HIDE IN SIGHT •

In this game the whole company must go out of the room, leaving only one. It is the business of this person to hide a coin—a quarter will do—only it must not be hidden out of sight. It should be put plainly in view, on a table or the back of a chair, but because the piece is small it will not readily be seen. The whole company is then ushered in and everybody begins to look for the coin—usually in the most improbable places. When one spies it he must not make any exclamation, must not even appear to have seen it, but must quietly go and sit down in a chair and say nothing.

The fun for that person then begins, as it is most entertaining to see how the different people take the discovery they have made. Almost everyone gives a little start when he sees it, then endeavors to look unconscious, strolls around the room once or twice, and then sits down. When everybody has found the quarter, of course everyone is seated. The last two or three have the worst of it because they are watched by all the rest, and the final one standing must pay a forfeit.

• NIP-NOSE •

Seat the party in a circle, ladies and gentlemen alternately as far as possible. One lady begins by gently taking the tip of her right-hand neighbor's nose between her thumb and finger, endeavoring by absurd questions and remarks to make him laugh or even smile.

If she succeeds, he pays a forfeit. In any case, he in turn bestows the same attention upon the lady at his right, she to the next gentlemen, and so on, all being bound, under penalty of a forfeit, to keep their countenances.

Of course, one would never think of preparing the tips of his fingers with burnt cork or carmine, whose transfer to a neighbor's nose would make him appear ridiculous, but it is, nevertheless, often done.

• MAGIC MUSIC •

One of the company takes a seat at the piano and another goes from the room. The remainder of the party then secretly hide some article previously agreed upon and recall the banished player.

At his entrance the pianist begins playing some lively air very softly, keeping up a sort of musical commentary upon his search, playing louder as he approaches the goal and softer when he wanders away from it.

In this way he is at last guided to the object of his search.

An interesting variation of this game is to have the company decide upon some act to be performed by the absent player upon his return: he must shake hands with a certain person in the room or sit in a certain chair, for example. By a little skill on the part of the pianist, this can be readily accomplished.

• THE RULE OF CONTRARY •

Standing up, all the players take hold of the sides of a handkerchief. The leader says, "When I say 'hold fast,' let go; when I say 'let go,' hold fast." He then says "let go" or "hold fast," as he may feel inclined. When he says "let go," those who do not hold fast pay forfeits; when he says "hold fast," all who do not immediately let go are punished in like manner.

• A COBWEB PARTY •

In preparation for this amusing pastime, two balls of string of contrasting colors are required, one color being for the ladies, the other for the gentlemen, and also as many gifts or favors (two of every kind) as the number of guests expected. Tie from the chandelier in the parlor the strings, and twine them around various articles of furniture, proceeding in a different direction with each string. They can be carried into other rooms, and even upstairs by twining around the banister. When the first strings have been carried far enough, break them from the balls, and to these ends attach favors. Then go back to the chandelier and tie other strings and make other goals by attaching favors, until there is the required number. The cobweb is then complete. When the guests have all assembled, and it is time to begin the game, they must gather around the chandelier, and to each one is given one of the strings. At a given signal, each member of the party begins following the course of his or her string, winding it into a ball as he or she proceeds toward the goal. As the favors are discovered, the finders return to the parlor. The gentlemen then search for the ladies holding corresponding favors to their own, and act as their escorts until after refreshments are served. Appropriate gifts are those which are sold as "German Favors," as these can be used in adorning the person, and thus afford a great deal of amusement.

• THE GAME OF TRUSSED FOWLS •

Two boys, having seated themselves on the floor, are trussed by their playmates; that is to say, each boy has his wrists tied together with a handkerchief and his legs secured just above the ankles with another; his arms are then passed over his knees, and a broomstick is pushed over one arm, under both knees, and out again over the other arm. The "trussed fowls" are now carried into the center of the room and placed opposite each other, with their toes just touching. The fun now begins, as each fowl endeavors, with the aid of his toes, to turn his antagonist over on his back or side, the one who can succeed in doing this winning the game. It frequently happens that both players are upset, and in that case, they must of course commence all over again.

• THROWING THE HANDKERCHIEF •

With the guests seated around the room in a circle, someone stationed in the center throws an unfolded handkerchief to one of the seated players.

Whoever receives it must instantly throw it to someone else, and so on, while the person in the center endeavors to catch the handkerchief in its passage from one player to another.

If he catches it as it touches somebody, that person must take his place in the center. If it is caught in the air, the player whose hands it last left enters the circle.

The handkerchief must not be knotted or twisted, but thrown loosely.

• THE GIANTESS •

Much amusement may be caused by performing the following:

A tall gentleman is dressed in a skirt. Then a large umbrella is covered over with a gown and cloak, a ball is secured on the tip of the umbrella above the dress, and a bonnet and a thick veil are put on it. The umbrella is partially opened, so that its frame sets out the dress and cloak as crinoline does. The gentleman goes under it and, holding the handle up as high as he can grasp, appears like a gigantic woman. Somebody knocks at the hall door, to pretend that there is an arrival, and a minute or two afterward the door is opened and "Miss Littlegirl" is announced. The Giantess then walks into the room to the amusement of the company.

A good effect is produced by holding the umbrella handle naturally when entering and then raising it by degrees, giving the appearance of a startling growth. She can thus appear to rise till she peers over the tops of pictures. She may talk to the company also, bending her head down toward them and speaking in a squeaking tone of voice.

• KI-YI •

This is rather a noisy game, but even older children enjoy a little romp occasionally. The game is played in the following manner:

The players stand and arrange themselves in two lines facing each other, as in the Virginia Reel. Everyone does simultaneously just as the leader does. He starts the game by singing, in a monotonous tone, "I turn my right hand in (suiting the action to the word by extending the hand toward his neighbor in the opposite line), I turn my right hand out (turning his body slightly around and extending a hand behind his back), I give my right hand a shake, shake, shake (shake hand), and turn my body about" (turn completely around). The leader turns around and, stepping between the two lines of players, marches to the end, followed by the other players. As they meet, they return in couples to their original places, all the while singing the following:

Ki, yi, yi, yi, yi
Ki, yi, yi, yi, yi
Ki, yi, yi
Ki, yi, yi,
Ki, yi, yi, yi, yi.

When the players are facing each other again, the leader starts with the left hand, all the foregoing being gone through with again.

The right foot is treated in the same way, then the left foot. The head is utilized by saying, "I put my head to the right, I put my head to the left, I give my head a shake, shake, shake, and turn my body around." At the end of every movement the march and the "Ki-Yi" are repeated. The head movement is the last. By the time this is reached, the company have had gymnastics and laughing enough to ensure a good night's sleep.

• BOSTON •

Seat the company around the room and give each a number.

Blindfold one person and station him in the center of the room, twirling him around several times so that he may successfully lose his bearings.

He must then call any two numbers assigned the players, and the two people representing them must at once rise and change places, while the "blind man" endeavors to seize one of them. If he succeeds in doing this, he must, while still blindfolded, identify the captive, who then, if identified, enters the circle.

More than two numbers may be called at once, and when the "blind man" calls out "Boston" and everybody changes places, he may, by slipping into a vacant seat during the confusion, when all the chairs are occupied find a surprised substitute in the person left standing.

• THE PROMENADE CONCERT •

The players seat themselves in a circle, each adopting a musical instrument on which he is supposed to be the performer. For instance, one may choose the violin, drawing his right hand backward and forward with a vigorous action as though he were drawing the bow across the instrument. Another, taking the cornet, puffs out his cheeks to the utmost extent. A third chooses a clarinet and rolls his eyes painfully. Another beats an imaginary drum, while still another, strumming with his hands upon his knees or a table (the latter real or imaginary), shows that the piano is his choice. The banjo, kazoo, flute, triangle, cymbal, tambourine, and trombone may all be represented. Every player must imitate the action and, as closely as possible, the sound peculiar to his adopted instrument, selecting any tune he may think best calculated to display its powers. No two players are allowed to play the same tune, and the greatest enthusiasm must be thrown into the performances.

The conductor takes his place in the center of the circle, sitting cross-legged on a chair, with his face to the back of another chair on which he beats time. When the "music" is at its height, and the greatest confusion prevails, the leader suddenly singles out one of the performers and asks him why he is at fault. The person thus unexpectedly pounced upon must immediately give some excuse for his want of accuracy, which excuse must be in keeping with the nature of his instrument. For instance, the fiddler replies that the bridge is broken, and he couldn't get across; the pianist, that he has left one of the keys of his instrument at home on his dressing table, and so on. Any delay in this, or repetition of an excuse already given, costs a forfeit.

• THE SILENT CONCERT •

In this performance, the guests for the time imagine themselves to be a band of musicians. The leader of the band is supposed to furnish each of the performers with a different musical instrument. Consequently a violin, a harp, a flute, a piano, a kazoo, and anything else, are all to be performed upon at the same time. The leader begins playing a tune on his imaginary cello, or whatever else it may be, imitating the way of performing it. The others all do the same, making for an exceedingly ludicrous spectacle. In the midst of it, the leader quite unexpectedly stops playing and makes an entire change in his attitude, substituting for his own instrument one belonging to someone else. As soon as he does this, the performer who has been deprived of his instrument takes the instrument of his leader and performs on it instead. Thus the game is continued, everyone expected to watch the leader's actions carefully, and to be prepared at any time to make a sudden change. Forfeits are, of course, in order when the player whose instrument has been appropriated fails to immediately imitate the motions that the leader has just abandoned.

• THE RIBBONS •

Forming a circle, each person in the company takes a ribbon, and holds it by one end. The other ends are all united in the hand of the one who leads the game, and who consequently is placed in the middle of the circle.

When he says "Pull" they must let go; when he says "Let go" they must pull the ribbon which they hold. It is astonishing how many forfeits are won at this simple game.

• BLIND MAN'S WAND •

A person is blindfolded and placed in the middle of the room, and a wand, light cane, or similar implement is given him. The players form a circle and dance around him, holding each other's hands, and singing any popular chorus. When the chorus is finished, all stand still, the "blind" person holds out his wand at hazard, and the person to whom it is pointed is obliged to take hold of it by the end presented to him. Then the "blind" player utters three cries, or sounds, which the holder of the wand is obliged to imitate. If the latter does not know how to disguise his voice, he is detected, and the blind player mentions his name and changes places with him.

• PORCO, BLIND MAN'S BUFF •

This game is similar to "Blind Man's Wand," in that several persons, male and female, join hands so as to form a circle, and one person, who is blindfolded, is placed in the center, with a small stick in his or her hand. The players dance around the blindfolded person, who tries to touch one of them with the wand. If he succeeds, the ring of people stops. The player then grunts like a pig—hence the name of the game—or crows like a rooster or imitates some other animal, and the person touched must try to imitate the noise as closely as possible, without revealing his or her identity. If the party touched is discovered, then the blindfolded player transfers the blindfold and stick to that player and takes the vacant place in the ring of persons, who once more resume their dance, until another player is touched.

• FRENCH BLIND MAN'S BLUFF •

In this game, instead of blindfolding one of the players, his hands are tied behind him, and in that difficult way he must try to catch one of his companions, who must, when caught, submit to the same restraint.

• BLIND MAN'S BUFF BY THE PROFILE •

When this game is played in a proper manner, it is very entertaining.

In this game, the "blind" player's eyes arc not bandaged, but he is nevertheless obliged to exercise all his acuity. A piece of white and rather fine linen is stretched upon a frame like a screen, in the same way as when exhibiting a magic lantern. The "blind" player is seated upon a stool, so low that his shadow is not represented upon the screen. Some distance behind him, a single lamp is placed upon a stand, and all the other lights in the room are extinguished.

When these arrangements are made, the rest of the company forms a kind of procession and passes in single file between the blind player (who is expressly forbidden to turn his head) and the table upon which the light is placed. This produces the expected effect; the light intercepted by each of the company in turn, casts upon the piece of white linen a succession of shadows quite accurately defined.

As these shadows move before him, the blind player is obliged to name aloud the person who he supposes is passing at the moment.

It is hardly necessary to say that each one, as he passes before the light, tries to disguise his attitude, his height, and his gait, to avoid being recognized.

It is not usual to give forfeits in this game, but still it would seem proper to demand them of those who are discovered. In this way it would probably afford entertainment to a greater number of players.

• BLIND MAN'S BUFF SEATED •

The players arrange themselves in a circle upon chairs placed very near together. The person chosen by lot, or who voluntarily offers to play the part of the "blind man," allows a handkerchief to be bound over his eyes.

When all are satisfied that the "blind man" cannot discern the objects that surround him, the players hastily change their places in order to baffle him. Then he approaches the circle without groping, for this is expressly forbidden, and seats himself in the lap of the first person he comes across. Without employing the sense of touch, but simply by listening to the stifled laughter around him, to the rustling of clothing, the sound of which often reveals the wearer, or perhaps by a fortunate guess, he is enabled to tell the name of the player upon whose lap he is seated, or, in case he is unacquainted with the person's name, to describe the player in such a manner that he or she can be recognized.

If the "blind man" guesses correctly, the person discovered takes his place, puts on the blindfold, and performs the same part. If, on the contrary, he is mistaken, the company clap their hands to inform him of his error, and he repeats the experiment in the same manner, without employing any other means than those authorized by the game.

It is customary for the company, in order to prevent the "blind man" from recognizing persons too readily, to resort to various little stratagems; for example, some may spread over their laps the skirts of their neighbors' dresses, while others might cover theirs with the cushions of the chairs. In any case, all try to disguise themselves in the best manner possible.

• THE WOLF AND THE HIND •

In this game, all the ladies present may be used, but only one gentleman is required, and the one who is considered the most agile should be chosen, for, in truth, he will find exercise enough for his dexterity and his patience.

This personage is called the Wolf; the eldest lady present is the Hind; all the others place themselves in a line behind her, according to their ages, and are called the Hind's fawns.

It is the Wolf's part to catch the lady who is at the extremity of the line, and he manifests his hostile intentions by the following conversation: "I am a Wolf, and I will eat you."

The Hind answers, "I am a Hind, and I will defend myself."

The Wolf replies, "I must have the youngest and tenderest of your fawns."

After this dialogue, the Wolf endeavors to seize the desired prey, but the Hind, extending her arms, keeps him off; but if he succeeds in passing her, the young lady at the end of the line may abandon her place before he can catch her, and place herself in front of the Hind, where she no longer runs any risk, and so with the rest in succession, until the Hind becomes the last of the line.

Then the game ends; the unskillful Wolf must pay as many forfeits as he has allowed young ladies to escape, and the players select a successor if they wish to renew the game.

If, on the contrary, before the end of the game, he succeeds in seizing one of the young fawns, he does not eat her, but he has a right to claim a kiss from her, and to make her pay a forfeit, which promises new pleasure at the end of the game.

Because it requires much quickness of movement and agility, this game is not as well suited for the house as for a lawn or field, where it presents a picturesque view to the onlookers, and at the same time enables the players to display to advantage the grace and rapidity of their movements.

• THE LEG OF MUTTON •

Almost everyone is acquainted with this game. The players place their fists alternately one upon the other, then the fist that is lowermost is withdrawn and placed on the top of the pile, each as he withdraws his fist counting one, two, and so on, to nine. As soon as the ninth fist is placed on the top, the whole pile is overturned, each hand being withdrawn as quickly as possible. The one who has pronounced the word "nine" must try to catch one of his companions by the hand, saying "This is my leg of mutton." If he fails to do this, he has to pay a forfeit. If he succeeds in catching a hand, he says to the player who has allowed himself to be caught, "Will you do one of three things?" If the player is polite, he simply answers, "I will, if I can." Others might reply, "I will, if I like." Then the winner gives him three things to do, and he performs either at his choice.

• HUNT THE SLIPPER •

This is usually an indoors game, although there is no other objection to its being played on a dry piece of turf than that the slipper cannot be heard, as struck by its momentary possessor when passing around the joyous ring. Several persons sit on the floor in a tight circle, shoulders touching, a slipper is given to them, and one, who generally volunteers to accept the office in order to begin the game, stands in the center. It is the latter's role to "chase the slipper by its sound." The parties who are seated pass it around so as to prevent, if possible, its being found in the possession of any individual. In order that the player in the center may know where the slipper is, it is occasionally tapped on the ground, and then suddenly handed on to the right or left. When the slipper is found in the possession of anyone in the circle by the player who is hunting it, the player on whom it is found takes the center position.

• THE CAT AND THE MOUSE •

All the players join hands in a circle, except one who is placed inside, called the Mouse, and another outside, called the Cat. The circle begins by dancing around, raising their arms. The Cat springs in at one side and the Mouse jumps out at the other; they then suddenly lower the arms so that the Cat cannot escape. The Cat goes around meowing, trying to get out; and as the circle must keep dancing around all the time, she must try to find a weak place to break through. As soon as she gets out, she chases the Mouse, who tries to save herself by getting within the circle again. For this purpose they raise their arms. If she gets in without being followed by the Cat, the Cat must pay a forfeit and try again; but if the Mouse is caught, she must pay a forfeit. Then the Cat and Mouse name who shall succeed them, join the circle, and the game goes on as before.

• HUNT THE HARE •

The players all form a circle, holding each other's hands. One, called the Hare, is left out and runs several times around the ring and at last stops, tapping one of the players on the shoulder. The one tapped quits the ring and runs after the Hare, the circle again joining hands. The Hare runs in and out in every direction, passing under the arms of those in the circle until caught by the pursuer, then he becomes the Hare himself. Those in the circle must always be friends to the Hare and assist its escape in every way possible.

• COPENHAGEN •

First procure a long piece of tape or twine, sufficient to go around the whole company, who must stand in a circle, holding in each of their hands a part of the string; the last takes hold of the two ends. One remains standing in the center of the circle. This one, who is called the Dane, must try to slap the hands of one of those who are holding the string, before they can be withdrawn. Whoever is not sufficiently alert, and allows the hands to be slapped, must take the place of the Dane and, in his turn, try to slap the hands of someone else.

• THE HUNTSMAN •

This game is one of the liveliest winter evening's pastimes that can be imagined. It may be played by any number of persons above four. One of the players is styled the Huntsman, and the others must be called after the different parts of the dress or accoutrements of a sportsman: thus, one is the coat, another the hat, while others portray the shot, shot-belt, powder, powder flask, dog, and gun, and every other appurtenance belonging to a huntsman. As many chairs as there are players, excluding the Huntsman, should next be arranged in two rows, back to back, and all the players must then seat themselves. The Huntsman walks around the sitters, and calls out the assumed name of one of them—for instance, "Gun!" That player immediately gets up and takes hold of the coattail of the Huntsman, who continues his walk, calling out all the others, one by one; each must take hold of the coattail of the player before him. When they are all summoned, the Huntsman sets off running around the chairs as fast as he can, the other players holding on and running after him. When he has run around two or three times, he shouts out "Bang!" and immediately sits down on one of the chairs, leaving his followers to scramble to the other seats as best they can. Of course, one must be left standing, there being one chair less than the number of players, and the player so left must pay a forfeit. The game is continued until all have paid three forfeits, when they are tried and the punishments or penances declared. The Huntsman is not changed throughout the game, unless he gets tired of his post.

• THE COTTON FLIES •

One of the players takes a flake of cotton or a bit of down, which he casts into the air in the midst of a circle formed by those present, who are seated close together. He at once puffs with his breath to keep it floating in the air, and the one toward whom the flake takes its course must puff in the same way to keep it from falling upon his lap, which would cost him a forfeit.

Nothing is more amusing than to see ten or twelve people, with upturned faces, blowing and puffing, each in his own way, to send from one to the other this flake of cotton. Sometimes it happens that because one cannot laugh and puff at the same moment, the tuft of cotton falls into the mouth of one of the company, who in vain tries to find breath enough to blow it away. This excites the laughter of the other players, who demand from him a forfeit for his gluttony.

• BLOWING PING-PONG BALLS •

Arrange the players with their hands behind them along the sides of a long extension table, down the center of which a row of Ping-Pong balls are placed at intervals of about two feet. Appoint two judges and place them at the ends of the table. At a given word, the players on both sides begin to blow the balls, endeavoring to blow them off their opponents' side of the table and to prevent any balls from being blown off their own side.

• STEPS •

A blindfolded player is placed in the middle of the room, and the other players all place themselves at various distances around him. The blindfolded player is then told how many steps he must take in order to be able to touch a certain player. This game does sound elementary in writing, but to try it is to find that it is not so easy as one imagines. It will also have the effect of making the dullest party lively, because the "blind man" makes such absurd mistakes as to the direction and length of steps that he has to take.

• PEANUT SHELLING •

Give each contestant ten peanuts, and at a signal let all begin to shell them, removing also the inner skin. The one who finishes first, without breaking the nut itself, wins. If a nut breaks into more than its two natural halves, another peanut must be shelled in its stead.

• PEANUT ROLLING •

Place peanuts across one side of the room at intervals of three feet, and give each contestant a toothpick. When the word is given, they commence to roll the peanuts across the room with the toothpicks. The one who first gets his peanut across the room is the victor. Another group of contestants then take their places in the same way. After all are through, the victors in the different contests have a final contest.

• PEANUT HUNT •

Peanuts are previously hidden in every conceivable place in the rooms to which the guests have access. The finder of the greatest number receives a prize.

• PROGRESSIVE PEANUT PARTY •

This is played exactly as are all other progressive games. Arrange tables to seat four, choose partners, and provide score cards.

In the center of each table, place a bowl containing one hundred peanuts in the shell, and lay a long common hatpin or a sturdy straightened paper clip at each place. At the head table have a bell. Before being seated to play, each guest is to have his right hand securely tied down to his side by a ribbon or fancy cord. When ready to commence, a player rings a bell at the head table, and all begin to spear nuts from the bowl; when the bowl is empty at the head table, the bell is rung and all count to see how many nuts they have. The two having made the best score progress to a winner's table while the others are matched together.

Five hundred may be the score limit, the winner being the one who first gets that number; or it may be decided to have the game end when the players at the head table, or at least two of them, return to that table.

• EMPTY HANDS •

Some member of the household produces a quantity of small cards. The number is not quite sufficient to supply the company, an intentional feature of the game. Four persons find themselves empty-handed when the bell rings. This bell is a signal for the passing, the object being to find someone without a card and rid oneself of the card in hand by passing it on. No one to whom a card is offered is allowed to refuse it, unless, of course, he already holds one. If empty-handed, he is obliged to receive the unwelcome gift and try to get rid of it as quickly as possible.

Each time the bell rings, which occurs at irregular intervals, making it impossible to calculate, the passing ceases, and all having empty hands win a point to count toward the final prize. Those having most points when the passing is over receive a prize.

• TURTLE •

Here is a game for those who have good, strong muscles. Any number may play, and the game commences by all sitting in a row resting their chins on their knees, and each holding his left ankle with his right hand and his right ankle with his left hand. This is a very difficult position to keep.

At a given signal, the turtles start for a goal a short distance away. The object of the game is to waddle to the goal and back to the starting point without removing one's hands from one's feet. The winner is, of course, the one who returns to the starting point first.

• AN OBSTACLE GAME •

Set stools, chairs, tables, or anything that is an obstacle in the most convenient place in the room; let those who are to take part in the game have two minutes to get their bearings. Then they leave the room and come back blindfolded. In the meantime, all the obstacles have been removed, but the warning cries of "Look out!" and the absurd attempts of the players to remember where the obstacles were make for great fun.

• ROLLING CHASE-BALL •

Two teams may play this game and two big balls or footballs are used. The teams line up in parallel rows, the players not facing each other, but behind one another and all facing the same way. The leader of each team holds a ball in both hands.

At the appointed signal, the leader, without bending his body or turning his head, tosses the ball backward to the player behind him. The ball is tossed backward again, and so passes along the line. The end player then runs to the head of the line, and the whole process is repeated again. The end player again goes to the front, and the game is continued until the original leader of the team is again at the head of his line. The team first reaching its order of formation wins the game.

It is essential that the ball should travel swiftly. Should any player drop the ball, he must run for it and regain his place in the line before passing it on. Should a toss be so strong as to pass above the player behind, so that he fails to receive the ball, the ball must be passed back so that the missed player shall handle it.

• A JAM-EATING CONTEST •

For this, thin slices of bread are spread with jelly or jam and placed upon a small plate at the edge of the table. Those who enter the contest must have their hands tied behind them, so that they are obliged to eat their bread and jam without touching it with a hand. The one who succeeds in disposing of his slice first receives a prize.

• A POTATO RACE •

Use peach baskets or the like for the goals. Potatoes, apples, or oranges are laid three feet apart in rows for the gathering contest. Each one must be picked up and carried on a spoon to the basket at the end of the row.

• HOME FIELD SPORTS •

- *One-Yard Dash.* This race consists in the attempt to push a penny a distance of a single yard across the floor by means of one's nose.
- *Tug of War.* A raisin is tied firmly in the middle of a long piece of twine, and each contestant takes a firm hold of one end of the twine in his mouth, and begins to chew his way along this string to reach the raisin. No one is allowed to use his hands.
- *Standing High Jump.* Three doughnuts are suspended in a doorway about four inches above the mouths of the jumpers. The contestants, with hands tied, attempt to take a bite. One bite from the doughnut wins a prize.
- *Hurdle Race.* The contestants take seats and thread six needles. The one who gets through first is the winner.
- *Drinking Race.* Each contestant is given a glass of water, which is to be absorbed by means of a spoon.
- *Bun Race.* Two poles are set up at a good distance apart, connected with a clothesline, from which are suspended strings of different lengths according to the height of each player, and a bun is tied to each string. The players line up, hands tied behind their backs, and at the signal each tries to eat his bun. The constant moving of the line caused by their efforts makes it almost impossible to get a bite. Soon a player gets a hold with his teeth, gets his bun on the ground, and, with his hands still behind, finishes the bun and gets the prize.
- *Cracker-Eating Contest* (for girls only). Girls choose sides and line up facing each other. Each girl has a

cracker, which she is to chew and swallow as quickly as possible. The side which has a girl able to whistle first wins the prize.

- *Rainy-Day Race.* This race is run by several players, who stand in a line with a closed satchel in front of each one, in which is a pair of overshoes, a pair of gloves, and also an umbrella. When "three" is counted, they open the satchels, take out the overshoes, put them on, take out the gloves, put them on, open their umbrellas, take the satchels, and walk (not run) about one hundred feet to a line. Here they lower the umbrellas, take off their gloves and overshoes, put them in the satchels, close them, and return, carrying the satchels and having the umbrellas closed. The first one back to the starting point wins. Other additions may be made.

• CUPID'S BOX •

The first player offers a box to his right-hand neighbor, saying, "I sell you my Cupid's Box, which contains three phrases—'To Love,' 'To Kiss,' 'To Dismiss.'" The neighbor answers, "Whom do you love? Whom do you kiss? Whom do you dismiss?"

At each of these questions, which are put separately, the person who has given the box names some individual present whom he loves, kisses, or dismisses. The person he kisses must in reality kiss him, and the one that he dismisses pays a forfeit. A player may love, kiss, or dismiss several, or even all, of those present; but this is permitted only once during the game, a rule that brings it to a termination.

• THE LAWYER •

The company forms in two rows, seated opposite to and facing each other, leaving room for the Lawyer to pass up and down between them.

The one who is the Lawyer will ask a question or address a remark to one of the company, either standing before the person addressed, or calling his name. The one spoken to must not answer, but the one sitting opposite him must reply to the question. The purpose of the Lawyer is to make either the one he speaks to answer him, or the one who should answer keep silent. He should therefore be rapid in moving from one to the next with his questions, taking them by surprise, as it were. No one must be allowed to remind another of his turn to speak. When the Lawyer has succeeded in either making one speak who should not, or finding any that did not answer when he should, he who had failed in his position pays a forfeit and must exchange places with the other, and the one caught becomes the Lawyer.

• SELLING STATUES •

A certain number of the players take the parts of statues and, as the artist may direct, stand at one end of the room, or seat themselves in a group.

The purchaser or purchasers then enter, and the artist proceeds to dispose of his works of art.

He covers the face of each statue for a moment with a light handkerchief as he describes it, removing the handkerchief again during his description.

The sale should be conducted along the lines of contraries, the descriptions being exactly opposite to the personal appearances, and no matter how absurd the variance, a smile or frown upon the face of the statue subjects the player to the penalty of a forfeit.

Example

In the studio we find Mr. Jones, of diminutive stature and insignificant features; Mrs. Thomson, a matron short but very stout, with florid complexion; Mr. Brown, very tall and large in build, and Miss Smith, a tiny blonde. Mr. Jackson, the artist, having arranged the statues, Mr. and Mrs. Hall enter to purchase.

Mr. Jackson. Good morning, sir. Pleased to see you, madam.

Mr. Hall. We have taken the liberty, Mr. Jackson, of calling to see what statues you have for sale.

Mrs. Hall. I want something classic for my front drawing room.

Mr. Jackson. Classic? Let me see. Have you seen my "Angry Jupiter"?

Mr. Hall. I have not seen it.

Mr. Jackson. (Throwing a handkerchief over the face of Mr. Jones.) There, you have still to behold one of the grandest creations of the nineteenth century (removing the handkerchief). The statue is colossal, four times the size of life, as we suppose Jupiter to have been built upon a grander scale than we mortals. Behold the grand proportions of the figure, that noble head, the massive features, and the magnificent pose of the shoulders. The personification of irresistible power!

Mrs. Hall. But, Mr. Jackson, such a ponderous statue would be out of place in my front parlor. You should sell it to some public park or hall. Show me something to fill a small niche in my flat.

Mr. Jackson. I fear that I have nothing else that is strictly classic. Would you like a Shakespearean subject? I have a much-admired statue here, a Titania (veils the face of Mrs. Thomson). This is a little gem, quite suitable for a bracket (removes handkerchief). As you perceive, it is upon a diminutive scale, as the subject demands. Observe the fairylike grace of the attitude, the tiny, graceful figure, the delicate features, and the sylphlike, ethereal proportions.

Mr. Hall. Have you anything historical?

Mr. Jackson. (Veiling Mr. Brown.) Napoleon the First. Proportioned by actual measurement, though one would hardly believe Napoleon was so small (removing the handkerchief.) The feet, especially, are like a lady's, and the whole power of this great man was concentrated in his brain. The head is large and noble.

Mrs. Hall. What is this, Mr. Jackson?

Mr. Jackson. Cleopatra (veiling Miss Smith), the
swarthy Egyptian, a specimen of the new art in statues (removing handkerchief). Like Jupiter, this
statue is on a large scale, but history assigns noble
proportions to Cleopatra. The jet hair and large eyes
suit well the bronze complexion.

The sale proceeds as far as the endurance of the statues
will last.

• INSECTS AND FLOWERS •

The players sit in a circle or in two rows, facing each
other, the gentlemen being together on one side, the ladies
on the other.

Each gentleman selects an insect that he is to impersonate,
a Wasp, Bee, Gnat, Fly, Hornet, Mosquito, or other insect.

The ladies each select a flower, such as a Rose, Violet,
Pink, Pansy, or any other flower.

One of the gentlemen selects a Butterfly, he being able to
relate an original story employing gardening language, the
continuation of which will form the game.

Whenever the narrator mentions the gardener, the insects
cover their faces with their hands, as if afraid, while the
flowers extend their arms.

When the watering can is mentioned, the flowers stand up
for a moment, as if refreshed, while the insects kneel down,
as if crushed.

When the sun is named, all rise and clap their hands three
times, as if pleased.

The moment an insect or flower is mentioned in the story, he or she must instantly continue the recital.

Never twice in the story must any insect or flower be called upon.

Forfeits are paid if any of the gestures are forgotten in their proper places, for any failure to answer to the assumed name, or for calling upon the same insect or flower who has already spoken.

Example

Butterfly. How glad I am that summer has come, when I can show my beautiful wings in the sun (all rise and clap their hands three times), and fly from flower to flower, enjoying their sweetness and beauty. I wonder if I have been forgotten by the beautiful white Lily during the winter?

Lily. Was not my name called, or have I imagined it? I thought I was mentioned by that odious Caterpillar.

Caterpillar. You may despise me now, vain flower, but remember that the brilliant insect who spoke your name was but lately a worm like myself. I have few friends in the garden. The gardener (ladies extend their arms, gentlemen hide their faces) spends hours trying to drive me from his flowers, for little they know of my devotion to the beautiful Rose.

Rose. How dare you, sir, speak of devotion to me, when the whole garden knows I am the betrothed bride of the Violet.

Violet. Was there ever such a vile slander! I am not
betrothed. I appeal to my friend, the Wasp.

Wasp. I will certainly bear testimony to your dis-
claimer. If the honorable member wishes for a flirta-
tion, I would refer him to that saucy little coquette,
the Pansy.

Pansy. Really, sir, your candor is overwhelming. Do you
for an instant imagine one of royal descent would
condescend to coquette? See my golden crown, my
purple robes, if you doubt my claim to kinship with
the aristocracy. But your sting is fatal, and I shall
appeal for protection to the valiant Hornet.

Hornet. To your rescue, gorgeous flower. How are we to
be insulted by plebeians, we of the nobility? Let me
but say farewell to my fair betrothed, the Camellia.

Camellia. I will never keep you from the field of
honor. . . .

And so the story passes from one to another, until each
has contributed a share.

• THE TINY ACTOR •

Two persons are required to enact the character of Dwarf.

Choose a deep window with full curtains, where there is
plenty of space for movement. A table is drawn to the window, and the curtains disposed so as to fall over the table,
and to conceal the person behind it. The player designated
the speaker proceeds to arrange himself in as gorgeous a

manner as possible, taking care to put on a loose jacket, with large sleeves. The arms must be dressed to represent legs, and the hands thrust into shoes or boots. The real origin of the legs is concealed by the jacket.

The second player takes his place behind the speaker, pushes his arms under the false legs of the speaker, and fits them carefully into the sleeves of the jacket. The speaker puts his hands on the table, and the curtain is then drawn and pinned up, so as to prevent anyone from seeing the performers. This part of the business is performed by other members of the company.

The spectators are admitted to the room.

The Dwarf, when everything is ready, begins a speech, interspersing it liberally with fantastic words and gestures. While he speaks, the actor performs the gestures, and herein lies the fun. The actor always tries to make his gestures wholly inappropriate to the language of the speaker, and indulges in all kinds of practical jokes.

• THE TRADES •

Each player is assigned a trade by a leader, and the players go through motions as if working at the trade assigned to him or her. For example, the shoemaker mends shoes; the washerwoman washes clothes; the painter paints a portrait; the cook kneads bread; the locksmith hammers upon an anvil; and the spinner turns her wheel.

One of the players, acting as King or Queen, begins the

game by working at his own trade. Meanwhile, all the others must make the movements appropriate to theirs. If the King suddenly changes his trade and takes up that of one of the company, all the rest must remain inactive, except the player whom the King is imitating, and he must at once take up the King's trade, until the latter is pleased to adopt another, then that player, in his turn, takes the King's trade, and all the rest remain idle until the King returns to his original trade, which is the signal for all present to take up their own trades.

If any one of the company makes a mistake, he pays a forfeit.

• MY LADY'S TOILET •

Place chairs for all the company except one. All are seated and have assumed the names of a lady's wardrobe and accessories, except the Lady's Maid, who stands in the center. The Lady's Maid now says, "My Lady's up, and wants her shoes." The one who has taken that name jumps up and calls "Shoes!," then sits down. If anyone does not rise as soon as called, he must pay a forfeit. If the Maid says, "My Lady wants her whole toilet," then everyone must jump up and change chairs, and because there is a chair too few, of course it occasions a scramble, and whoever is left standing must take the part of the Lady's Maid.

• SCISSORS CROSSED OR NOT CROSSED •

EACH PLAYER in his turn "passes" to his neighbor a pair of scissors, or any other object, saying, "I give you my scissors crossed (or "not crossed")."

If the former, the player, as he utters the words, must cross his arms or his feet in a natural manner. If the latter, he must be careful to keep them separate. The person who receives the scissors must be careful to imitate this action. Many persons, from mere want of attention, render themselves liable to forfeits in this game, and without knowing why. Their surprise produces the chief part of the amusement.

• THE DIVINER •

The point of this game consists in divining or guessing a word that is named in the midst of several others. Two players, in order to trick a third, commonly agree to place it after an object that, for instance, has four legs, such as a quadruped or a table.

Example

Two conspiring players, Emily and Henry, wish to dupe Susan. Emily wishes to have Henry guess the word that Susan has secretly told her, so she says to him, "Susan has been shopping; she has bought a rose, a dress, some jewelry, a table, a bonnet, a shawl."

Henry of course will easily guess that the object in question is a bonnet, for the word "table," which precedes it, has four legs.

• THE CHERRIES •

Each of the company takes the name of a fruit: Pear, Apricot, Peach, Plum, etc., and all sit making a circle.

A basket of cherries, with their long stems, is placed on a table.

Then the leader says, "Who will have some cherries?" Each one replies, "I will," and takes one from the basket.

The company then take their seats, except the leader, who stands in the middle of the circle and says, "I should like to exchange my cherry for a pear," or any other fruit he chooses to name, which may have been selected by the players. The one who has taken the name of Pear must answer immediately, "I have got a pear." "Well, then," says the leader, "give me your pear and I will give you my cherry." "How will you have it?" replies the person thus addressed, "by the fruit or by the stem?" Let us suppose the questioner says, "By the fruit." In that case the other has several ways of obeying. He may place the stem in his mouth and let the cherry be taken from it, or put it in his hair, or in his slipper, or under a candlestick.

There is still another way of replying to the words "By the fruit," such as to throw the cherry in his face. Then, confused and mortified, he replies, "This pear is not ripe." He then pays a forfeit and renews his questions, naming another fruit that he chooses, and with the same results.

Sometimes, instead of wishing to have it by the fruit, the questioner asks to have it by the stem. Then the other, holding the cherry between his fingers, offers the stem of the fruit and lets him take it.

Instead of holding it between his fingers, he puts the cherry in his mouth and the questioner seizes it by the stem, but to no purpose, since the cherry becomes detached and the other swallows it, leaving him the stem, disappointing him, and claiming a forfeit in the bargain. His only resource then is to offer to exchange his cherry for some other fruit, when the person who has taken this fruit for his name tries to entrap him in the same way.

• RIGHT IS WRONG •

Begin by standing exactly opposite a person and gravely informing him that he cannot imitate you in actions of the simplest description without making mistakes.

To show that the movements are easy, go through them as follows: Hold your left arm well forward, with an extended forefinger, draw an imaginary circle around your face, accompanying the action with the words "The earth is round"; then point to each of your eyes, saying, "Two eyes";

then touch the point of your nose, saying, "A nose"; and finally point to your mouth, saying, "And a mouth."

You now challenge the person opposite you to go through the same routine without a mistake. Unless he is left-handed, he is almost sure to perform the action with his right hand, which will allow you to tell him that it is all wrong. He may repeat it many times over without discovering in what the error exists; he will fail to see that the "right" is "wrong." Should he, however, use his left hand, you may say, "Now try again, and this time watch my motions very closely," repeating the motions with your right hand.

• THE ANTEATERS •

A sure way to raise a laugh among a party of friends is to claim that you can do an apparently impossible thing, and then get your friends to try it; then, when they have tried and failed, do the very thing they failed at in a simple way that has never occurred to them. Here is a deception that seldom fails to work, and which always provides a lot of fun, even to those who are fooled by it.

Begin by saying something about anteaters, which have such long tongues that they can touch the ground with them without lowering their heads, and then ask one of your friends if he can put out his tongue and touch his ear. He will try, gently at first, then harder, and at length make the funniest faces by trying to do a thing that is, of course, impossible. Then others will try poking their tongues out of the corners of their mouths, and trying to curl them around their cheeks until their ears are reached.

When they have finished, you put out your tongue, and touch your ear with your finger.

• GYMNASTICS FOR THE TONGUE •

Say these sentences several times as rapidly and distinctly as you can: "She sells sea shells at the sea shore," and these also: "John sawed six sleek, slim, slender saplings." "There was an old woman and she was a thistle sifter. She had a sieve of sifted thistles, and a sieve of unsifted thistles, and she was a thistle sifter." "Mixed biscuits." "Gig whip." "Six thick thistle sticks." "She stood at the door welcoming him in." "Shoes and socks shock Susan."

• SURPRISING STRENGTH •

Lightly put the tips of the fingers of both hands together. If you invite anyone to separate them by taking your wrists and trying to draw them apart in a direct line with each other, they will be surprised to find that no amount of strength will avail them at all, as the thing is really almost impossible to do.

Place your clenched fists one upon the other, and ask someone to separate them by pushing them aside. They will be quite unable to do so, although you are exerting your strength but little against them.

Let them, however, approach you with their forefingers only, and give a sharp rap at your knuckles in opposite directions. You will find that you are quite powerless against this, and cannot keep your fists together at all.

• I HAVE JUST COME FROM SHOPPING •

The company forms a circle, and one of the party says to her right-hand neighbor, "I have just come from shopping."

"What have you bought?" asks the latter. "A robe, a vest, stockings, flowers"—in fact, anything that comes into the purchaser's head, provided that in uttering the words she can touch an object similar to the one she names. Those who follow but neglect to do the same must pay a forfeit; a forfeit can be required also from anyone who names an object that has been named by any player previously.

• THE MOLE •

This simple game consists merely in asking one of the players, "Have you seen my mole?"

The latter answers, "Yes, I have seen your mole."

"Do you know what my mole is doing?"

"Yes, I do know what your mole is doing."

"Can you do as it does?"

The person who replies must shut his eyes at each answer; if he fails to do so he pays a forfeit.

• THE COOK WHO LIKES NO PEAS •

The leader of the game must put the following question to his right-hand neighbor, and then to all the players in succession:

"My cook likes no peas—what shall I give her to eat?"

If any player replies, "Potatoes, parsnips," the other answers, "She does not like them; pay a forfeit."

But if another says, "Onions, carrots, veal, chickens," she likes them, and consequently no forfeit is required of the player.

The trick of this game is evident. It is the letter p that must be avoided. Thus, to escape the penalty of a forfeit, it is necessary that the players should propose some kind of vegetable or food in which the letter p does not occur, such as beans, radishes, venison, and so on.

• THE GAME OF CAT •

The person who is to play the part of Cat should stand outside the door of the room where the company is assembled. The boys and girls, in turn, come to the other side of the door and call out "meow."

If the Cat outside recognizes a friend by the cry, and calls out his name correctly in return, Cat is allowed to enter the room and embrace the player, and the latter then takes the place of Cat.

If, on the contrary, Cat cannot recognize the voice, he is hissed by the miscalled player, and remains outside until he is able to do so.

• THE FARMYARD •

This game, if carried out properly, will cause great amusement. One of the party announces that he will whisper to each person the name of some animal, which, at a given signal, must be imitated as loudly as possible. Instead of giving the name of an animal to each, however, he whispers to all the company, with the exception of one, to keep perfectly silent. To that one he whispers that the animal he is to imitate is the donkey.

After a short time, so that all may be in readiness, the signal is given. Instead of all the party making the sounds of various animals, nothing is heard but a loud bray from the one unfortunate member of the company.

• WHAT'S O'CLOCK? •

Ask any person to think of some hour of the day and that you will guess it correctly. Tell him to subtract his chosen hour from twenty and remember the remainder, keeping it to himself. Take out your watch and inform him that you are going to count around on the dial, and that when you have counted the number corresponding with the remainder that he was to remember, he must stop you. For instance, suppose he thought of five o'clock. Five taken from twenty leaves fifteen. You now count randomly, but not aloud, pointing at each count with a pencil to any one of the hours on the dial, but taking care at the eighth count to point to the seven, and thence in rotation counterclockwise. When you come to five o'clock you will be stopped, as this will be the fifteenth count, corresponding to the remainder, fifteen, which he was to remember. You will thus know that five o'clock was the hour thought of.

• THE LITTLE FORTUNE-TELLER •

This game is played by any number of persons, and produces much amusement. The person who wishes to try his fortune must place his finger on the board without looking; then refer to the list for the number marked on the square touched, and read his fortune.

117	18	119	120	121	82	83	84	85	86	87
116	78	79	80	81	50	51	52	53	54	88
115	77	47	48	49	26	27	28	29	55	89
114	76	46	24	25	10	11	12	30	56	90
113	75	45	23	9	2	3	13	31	57	91
112	74	44	22	8	1	4	14	32	58	92
111	73	43	21	7	6	5	15	33	59	93
110	72	42	20	19	18	17	16	34	60	94
109	71	41	40	39	38	37	36	35	61	95
108	70	69	68	67	66	65	64	63	62	96
107	106	105	104	103	102	101	100	99	98	97

• ANSWERS TO THE LITTLE FORTUNE-TELLER •

1. A life full of changes—die rich.
2. Early marriage and prosperity.
3. You will have many lovers, but die single.
4. A speedy journey of great importance.
5. Become rich through a legacy.
6. Hours of pleasure, years of care.
7. Your present lover is false.
8. You will marry your present choice.
9. Wed thrice, and die in widowhood.
10. You will travel over land and sea.
11. If not already wed, you never will be.
12. You will meet with great disappointment.
13. You will be very happy in marriage.
14. You will change your love soon.
15. A long and prosperous life.
16. A rival will cause you tears.
17. Beware of a false friend.
18. Fate decrees you two partners.
19. You will be very happy though poor.
20. You will not wed your present lover.
21. You will fall desperately in love.
22. You will soon be in mourning.
23. You will gain an estate by industry.
24. You will better yourself by marriage.
25. You will lose money by fraud.
26. You will marry an ill-tempered person.
27. A sudden raise attends you.

28. An absent lover will return.
29. You will have enemies, but you will overcome them.
30. A bad partner, but happy reformation.
31. A speedy proposal of marriage.
32. A handsome present.
33. You will be invited to a blithesome party.
34. A serious quarrel.
35. A new lover.
36. A run of ill luck.
37. Gifts of money.
38. A good partner in marriage.
39. You will become rich.
40. Money through love.
41. Cash by trade.
42. A long journey.
43. Important news soon.
44. A threatening letter.
45. A present from a distance.
46. A dispute with one you love.
47. A visit from a distant friend.
48. A lawsuit.
49. Advancement in life.
50. Love at first sight.
51. A prize worth having.
52. Wealth, dignity, honor.
53. A visit to a foreign land.
54. Profit by industry.
55. A multitude of cares.
56. Preferment through a friend.
57. Your second partner will be better than your first.

58. You will surmount many difficulties.
59. A false friend.
60. A pleasing surprise.
61. A change in your affairs.
62. A ramble by moonlight.
63. You will be injured by scandal.
64. Unpleasant tidings.
65. Great loss and disappointment.
66. You are about to attend a christening.
67. Change of situation.
68. A handsome present from an unknown bearer.
69. An invitation to a marriage.
70. News from sea.
71. Happiness or marriage.
72. Pleasant intelligence from abroad.
73. A life of single blessedness.
74. You are in love, though you won't admit it.
75. You will quarrel with your intended.
76. Disappointment in love.
77. You will fall in love with one who is already engaged.
78. You will soon fall heir to an estate.
79. An unexpected death.
80. You meditate an elopement.
81. A dangerous illness.
82. Crosses and disappointments await you.
83. You have three strings to your bow.
84. You long to be married.
85. Your intended is in the sere and yellow leaf.
86. A lowly home and a happy heart.
87. You will marry a widow (or widower).

88. You will have many friends.
89. You will be married this year.
90. Marry in haste and repent at leisure.
91. You will be apt to break your promise.
92. You are in danger of losing your sweetheart.
93. Beware of changing for the worse.
94. You shall have many offers.
95. You will be happy and contented.
96. You will shortly obtain your wishes.
97. An advantageous bargain.
98. You will see your intended next Sunday for the first time.
99. Others will covet your good luck.
100. You will travel in a foreign land.
101. Venture freely and you will certainly gain.
102. Your present speculations will succeed.
103. You love one who does not love you.
104. Wealth will come from a quarter you little suspect.
105. You will obtain your wishes through a friend.
106. A fortune is in store for you; persevere.
107. Alter your intention; you cannot succeed.
108. Remain at home for the present.
109. Ill luck awaits you.
110. Prepare for a journey.
111. You will succeed according to your wishes.
112. Beware of persons who seek to do you harm.
113. Misfortune at first, but comfort and happiness after.
114. Prosperity in all your undertakings.
115. Rely not on one who pretends to be your friend.
116. Change your situation and you will do better.

117. It will be difficult for you to get a partner.
118. Your lover is whimsical and changeable.
119. You will meet with sorrow and trouble.
120. You will receive a telegram containing good news.
121. Your marriage will be a disappointment.

FORFEITS

BY MANY people of the present day, forfeits, such a fitting termination to an evening of games, are considered childish and absurd. So it may be if the penalties are confined to "kissing the one you love best" or "singing in one corner, crying in another, and dancing in another." But there are forfeits that are not only amusing, but worthy of the approval of the most conventional.

One method is to require each person present to write out a penalty upon paper. These, being collected, are drawn one at a time by the sentenced players as required, the forfeits for ladies and gentlemen being distinguished by being written upon different-colored papers.

Another method is this: Forfeits, it will be seen, have each a separate name and number. A good plan would be for a person who is to take an active part in the evening party to read them over during the day and to become acquainted with them. Then, in allotting the forfeits, when they are called, thus:

"Here's a pretty thing, and a very pretty thing, and what shall the owner of this thing do?"

The person awarding the forfeits may call out "Number 1," "Number 10," "Number 15," or any other number; or may say (which would be more amusing), "Hush-a-bye, Baby!" "Hobson's Choice!" "Dot and Carry One!" and so on. This work may be laid on the table, to afford further explanation of the forfeits, or be held in the hand of the person who is holding up the forfeits while they are being cried; and this person can at once explain what is to be done. In this way the redemption of the forfeits will go on freely, without stopping or hesitation, and a capital evening's amusement be derived.

• 1. MAKING A CARD DANCE ON THE WALL •

Give the culprit a blank card, telling him that if he will obey directions and place it in the proper position, you will make it execute a dance upon the wall. Then bid him place it upon a certain spot—a little farther to the right—not quite so far—a little higher—higher yet—now a trifle to the left—a little lower and to the right. Perhaps by this time he will begin to realize that he is the victim of a joke, and that it is he himself who is making the card "dance upon the wall."

• 2. THE BROOM AND HANDKERCHIEF FEAT •

Place two chairs of equal height facing each other, and across their seats, which must be two or three feet apart, rest a broom.

On each corner of both chair-backs, loosely suspend a handkerchief. Seating the victim upon the handle of the broom between the chairs, with his feet held above the floor, give him a cane and bid him knock off the four handkerchiefs without touching his feet or hands to anything for support.

If the person is in great danger of falling the cane may be rested upon the floor for an instant to regain equilibrium.

• 3. TOUCHING A MARK •

Blindfold the culprit and lead him toward a spot on the wall (previously designated), and tell him to endeavor to place his finger upon it. As he stretches out his finger to do so, quickly step in front of him and catch his finger between your teeth.

• 4. WALKING TOPPER •

The person under sentence is stationed either at one end of a long room or in a room with double doors, facing the doors. In either case, care should be taken to remove all the furniture from his vicinity.

A cane is given him, and he is instructed to rest it upon the floor, put both hands on top of it, and, bending over, rest his forehead upon his hands.

In this position he must turn around three times, and then, standing erect, walk straight ahead without pausing to collect himself.

His endeavors to "keep straight" will rival those of the most hopeless inebriate.

• 5. A DRY REPAST •

Spread a sheet upon the floor and place two chairs upon it. Seat the culprits in the chairs within reach of each other, and blindfold them.

Give each a saucer of cracker or bread crumbs and a spoon, then request them to feed each other. The frantic efforts of each victim to reach his fellow sufferer's mouth is truly absurd—the crumbs finding lodgment in the hair, ears, and neck much oftener than the mouth. Sometimes bibs are fastened around the necks of the victims for protection.

• 6. A BIG SNEEZE •

This is a triple forfeit, and requires that the three culprits stand in a line while the judge gives to one the syllable "hish," to the second "hash," and to the third "hosh."

Then, at a given signal, the syllables must be uttered together in most stentorian tones. The result is a good imitation of a genuine sneeze.

The effect is heightened if all the people in the room are called upon to share the penalty and are divided into three groups, each group giving one of the syllables to be uttered.

• 7. BLOWING OUT A CANDLE •

Light a candle and place it upon a table. Blindfold the culprit, station him with his back to the candle, directly before it, and tell him to take three steps forward, turn around three times, and walk back three steps in the direction of the candle, which he must then endeavor to blow out.

Perhaps he will—but again, perhaps he will endeavor to extinguish something or somebody in an entirely different part of the room.

• 8. THE TONGUE TEASER •

Repeat the following sentence five times rapidly: Villy Vite and his wife vent to Vest Vinsor and Vest Vickham on Vednesday.

• 9. WILLIAM TELL •

The person to be punished has his hands tied tightly together at the wrists with a handkerchief. Somebody who has been previously initiated, and who should be taller than the culprit, represents Tell's son, with a knotted handkerchief upon his head to serve as an apple. Tell is then requested to advance and, with his pinioned hands, knock the apple from the head of his son.

As he elevates his arms for this purpose, the son quickly thrusts his head between them and, standing erect, appears to be embraced by Tell, from which embrace the astonished father is unable to release himself until the company has sufficiently enjoyed his situation.

• 10. TO PICK UP A CARD WITHOUT TOUCHING IT •

Bend an ordinary visiting card so that, when resting upon the floor, half of it will be in a perpendicular position.

Bid the victim to kneel and, placing his elbow against his knees, stretch out his arm at full length upon the floor. Where his fingertips rest, place the card with the upright part next to him, and then with both hands behind his back he must pick up the card with his teeth.

• 11. PRINCESS HUGGER-MUGGER •

The two players are stationed at opposite sides of the room, facing each other, and each holding a lighted candle. They advance slowly, their eyes fixed firmly upon each other's faces, until they meet in the center of the room, when the following dialogue occurs:

Player 1. "The Princess Hugger-Mugger is dead. Dead, defunct, and gone."

Player 2. "Is she? When did she die?"

Then they slowly retreat backwards to their original position. Each must try, by grimaces and whatever artifice he chooses, to draw a smile from the other, and the performance is repeated until both can go through it with perfect solemnity.

• 12. THREADING A NEEDLE •

Place a champagne bottle or large olive bottle on its side. Seat the culprit upon the bottle, with the heel of his right foot resting upon the ground and the heel of his left upon the toe of the right. Then give him a moderately large needle and a piece of thread, and laugh at his effort to pass the thread through the eye of the needle without changing his position or falling off his insecure seat.

• 13. VOWELS •

Require that the person under sentence answer five questions asked him by different members of the party without using words containing certain vowels designated by the questioners.

Example

Player 1. Why did you come here tonight? Answer without *a*.

Player 2. For fun.

Player 3. When are you going home? Answer without *e*.

Player 2. Not until I wish.

• 14. PICKING UP A COIN •

Place the player with his back to the wall and his heels close together, touching the baseboard. Then bid him pick up a coin laid on the floor before him without moving his heels, offering the coin as a reward if he succeeds.

• 15. THE KNIGHT OF THE RUEFUL COUNTENANCE •

The forfeiting player must take a lighted candle in his hand and select some other player to be his squire, who takes hold of his arm, and they then both go around to all the ladies in the company. It is the squire's office to kiss the hand of each lady, and after each kiss to wipe the knight's mouth with a handkerchief. The knight must carry the candle through the penance, and preserve a grave countenance.

• 16. JOURNEY TO ROME •

The person whose forfeit is called must go around to all in the company, to tell them that he is going on a journey to Rome, and that he will feel great pleasure in taking anything for His Holiness the Pope. Everyone must give something to the traveler. (The more cumbersome or awkward to carry, the more fun it occasions.) When he has gathered all, he is to carry the things to one corner of the room and deposit them, and thus end his penance.

• 17. LAUGHING GAMUT •

Sing the laughing gamut without pause or mistake, thus:

```
                            ha
                ha                    ha
                  ha                    ha
                 ha                      ha
              ha                      ha
                ha                          ha
     ha                              ha
     ha                                      ha
```

• 18. THE MEDLEY •

Sing one line of four different songs without pausing
between them. It would be well to find four lines that afford
humor, taken consecutively, such as the following:

"All around my hat."

"A rare old plant is the ivy green."

"Sweet Kitty Clover, she bothers me so."

"In the Bay of Biscay, O."

• 19. HOBSON'S CHOICE •

Burn a cork on one end, and keep it clean on the other. The
culprit is blindfolded, and the cork is held horizontally to
him and turned several times until he says "Hobson." Then
that end of the cork must be passed along his forehead; the

cork must then be turned again, and whichever end he stops next must be passed down the nose; and the third time, across his cheeks or chin. He is then to be allowed to see the success of his choices.

This will afford capital fun, and should be played fairly, to give the person who owns the forfeit a chance of escape. The end of the cork should be thoroughly well burnt. As a joke for Christmas, this is perfectly allowable, and the damp corner of a towel or handkerchief will set all right. It should be allotted to a gentleman, and one who has a good broad and bare face.

• 20. POETIC NUMBERS •

Repeat a passage of poetry, counting the words aloud as you proceed thus:

Full (one) many (two) a (three) flower (four) is (five) born (six) to (seven) blush (eight) unseen (nine) and (ten) waste (eleven) its (twelve) sweetness (thirteen) in (fourteen) the (fifteen) desert (sixteen) air (seventeen)! This will prove a great puzzle to many, and afford considerable amusement.

• 21. HUSH-A-BYE BABY •

Yawn until you make several others in the room yawn.

(This can be done well by one person who can accurately imitate yawning, and it will afford indescribable mirth. It should be allotted to one of the male sex, with a large mouth and a somber or heavy appearance, if such a one can be found in the party.)

• 22. THE BEGGAR •

A penance to be inflicted on gentlemen only. The penitent takes a staff, and approaches a lady. He falls on his knees before her and, thumping his staff on the ground, implores "Charity." The lady, touched by the poor man's distress, asks him, "Do you want bread?" "Do you want water?" "Do you want a penny?" and so on. To all questions such as these, the Beggar replies by thumping his staff on the ground impatiently. At length the lady says, "Do you want a kiss?" At these words the Beggar jumps up and kisses the lady.

• 23. THE PILGRIM •

The Pilgrim is very like the Beggar. A gentleman conducts a lady around the circle, saying to each member of it, if a gentleman, "A kiss for my sister, and a morsel of bread for me." If a lady, "A morsel of bread for my sister, and a kiss for me." The bread is of no particular importance, but the kiss is indispensable.

• 24. THE EGOTIST •

Toast your own health in a complimentary speech, and sing accompanying musical honors.

• 25. DOT AND CARRY ONE •

Hold one ankle in one hand, and walk around the room. (This is suited only to gentlemen.)

• 26. THE IMITATION •

If a gentleman, he must put on a lady's bonnet, and imitate the voice of the lady to whom it belongs; if a lady, then a gentleman's hat, etc. Sometimes these imitations are very humorous. A sentence often used by the person imitated should be chosen.

• 27. GOING TO SERVICE •

Go to service; apply to the person who holds the forfeits for a place, for example as "maid of all work." The questions then to be asked are "How do you wash?" "How do you iron?" "How do you make a bed?" "How do you scrub the floor?" "How do you clean knives and forks?" The whole of these processes must be imitated by the culprit with appropriate motions, and if the replies are satisfactory, the forfeit must be given up.

• 28. KISSING THE CANDLESTICK •

When ordered to kiss the candlestick, you politely request a lady to hold the candle for you. As soon as she has it in her hand, she is supposed to be the candlestick, and you, of course, kiss *her*.

• 29. THE DISAPPOINTMENT •

A lady advances toward the penitent, as if to kiss him, and when close to him she turns quietly around and allows the expected kiss to be taken by her nearest neighbor.

• 30. THE FLORIST'S CHOICE •

Choose three flowers, for example, Pink, Fuchsia, and Lily. Two of the party must then privately agree to the three persons of the forfeiter's acquaintance each to be represented by one of the flowers. Then proceed: What will you do with the Pink? Dip it in the water! What with the Fuschia? Dry it, and keep it as a curiosity! With the Lily? Keep it until it is dead, then throw it away! The three names identified with the flowers are now to be told, and their fates will excite much merriment.

• 31. THE FOOL'S LEAP •

Tell the culprit, "Put two chairs back to back, take off your shoes, and jump over them." (The fun consists in a mistaken idea that the *chairs* are to be jumped over, whereas it is only the *shoes*!)

• 32. TO KISS THE ONE YOU LOVE BEST WITHOUT ITS BEING NOTICED •

Kissing all the ladies in the company one after another without any distinction.

• 33. THE GUESS BY SPOON •

The person who owns the forfeit is to be blindfolded; a glass of water and a teaspoon are then to be brought, and a spoonful given alternately by the members of the company until the person blindfolded guesses aright.

• 34. THE EXILE •

The penitent sent into exile takes up his position in the part of the room most distant from the rest of the company, with whom he is forbidden to communicate. From there he is compelled to fix the penance to be performed by the owner of the next forfeit, till the accomplishment of which he may on no account leave his place. This may be prolonged for several turns. The last penitent, as soon as he has acquitted himself satisfactorily, takes the place of the exile, and passes sentence on the next.

• 35. THE "B" HIVE •

Repeat, without stopping:

Bandy-Legg'd Borachio Mustachio Whiskenfusticus
the bold and brave Bombardino of Baghdad
helped Abomilique Blue Beard Bashaw of Babelmandeb
to beat down a bumble bee at Balsora.

• 36. ROB ROWLEY •

Repeat the following:

Robert Rowley rolled a round roll round,
A round roll Robert Rowley rolled round,
Where is the round roll Robert Rowley rolled round?

• 37. THE STATUE OF LOVE •

The player who must pay the forfeit takes a candle in his hand and is led by another to one end of the room, where he must stand and represent the Statue of Love. One of the players now walks up and requests him to fetch some lady, whose name he whispers in Love's ear; the Statue, still holding the candle, proceeds to execute his commission, and brings the lady with him. She in turn desires him to fetch some gentleman, and so it continues until all have been summoned. The players brought up by Love must not return to their seats, but stand in a group around Love's standing-place until he has brought the last person in the company, upon which they hiss him most vigorously, and the forfeit terminates.

• 38. THE CHANCE KISS •

The penitent takes from a pack of cards the four kings and the four queens, shuffles them, and, without looking at them, distributes them to a proportionate number of ladies and gentlemen. The gentleman finding himself possessed of the king of hearts kisses the lady holding the queen, and so on with the rest.

• 39. THE BLIND QUADRILLE •

This is performed when a great number of forfeits are to be disposed of. A quadrille is danced by eight of the company with their eyes blindfolded, and as they are certain to become completely bewildered during the figures, it always affords infinite amusement to the spectators.

• 40. THE TURNED HEAD •

This penalty should be imposed upon a lady, who is dressed with as many wrappings as possible, but every cloak, shawl, victorine, etc., is to be put on backwards, so as to present the appearance of a "turned head." She should be furnished with a muff, which she must hold behind her as much as possible in the usual manner, but her bonnet must be put on in the proper way. Thus equipped, she must enter the room walking backwards and, until her punishment is at an end, must continue to move in the same way.

• 41. THE KING OF MOROCCO IS DEAD •

The culprit takes a candle in his hand and, stepping forward, places another candle in the hands of a person of a different sex; then both march to opposite sides of the room. They then assume a mournful air and advance toward each other with a slow and measured step. When they meet, they raise their eyes to the ceiling, utter some words in a sepulchral tone, and then, with downcast eyes, march on, each to take the place occupied by the other.

• 42. THE STATUE MAKERS •

The culprit stands on a chair and is posed as a living statue by members of the company in succession according to their various and sometimes very original conceptions, such as placing the head, shutting one eye, opening the mouth, placing the arm, hand, or foot to suit the fancy, or making him assume any position.

• 43. PHYSICAL FORFEITS •

The following forfeits can be allotted gentlemen or ladies, though consideration should be taken, as they require nimbleness and physical acuity. Their enacting causes great amounts of laughter at the culprit, but some are surely unfit for all persons when proper convention is in order.

Grasp the right ankle by the right hand and, standing on the left leg, bend it until the right knee touches the floor, then rise slowly to a standing position again. The left hand must be kept extended all the time and must touch nothing. The right foot must not be allowed to touch the floor, nor the ankle released from the right hand.

Instruct the culprit to put one hand where the other cannot touch it. (This is performed by grasping the right elbow with the left hand.)

Place an object on the floor in such a manner that no one can jump over it. (This is done by placing it close against the corner.)

Place a stool on the floor against a wall. Stand away from the wall twice the width of the stool. Stoop down and seize the stool by the top in both hands and place the top of your head against the wall, your back being almost horizontal. Lift the stool from the ground without assistance, or try, at any rate.

These are but a few of the many forfeits that can be devised with trifling ingenuity. If the mental caliber of the company warrants it, call for extemporaneous speeches or poems, conundrums on given subjects—anything that the mind of the judge can conceive—only never regard forfeits as obsolete and ready to be laid upon the shelf for lack of fresh material.